[VIDEO] KLAPPE

Kate Pelling

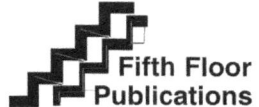

Fifth Floor
Publications

[VIDEO] KLAPPE
By Kate Pelling
Published by Fifth Floor Publications, London, UK and Frankfurt am Main, Germany
Copyright 2014 Fifth Floor Publications and Kate Pelling

ISBN 978-0-9576128-1-5

INTRODUCTION

In the last few years I have been obsessed with editing processes. Video editing techniques, speech production and linguistic editing processes, transcription, translation, a variety of forms of drawing, text editing, and editing processes towards publication. *[Video] Klappe* embodies the next stage in my obsession – editing my [video] environment.

So, what is my [video] environment? I am using this term to describe the space in front of the video camera that will be captured by the recording. This space belongs to the video process and is limited by the scope of the camera lens. My definition of [video] environment also extends to the recorded image of the space, which is artificially framed by the video process. For clarification, my [real] environment has a considerably broader remit and includes all of my surroundings, regardless of whether there is a camera present or not. However, my [real]

EINLEITUNG

Seit einigen Jahren bin ich von Bearbeitungsvorgängen besessen. Videobearbeitungstechniken, Sprachproduktion und linguistische Bearbeitungsprozesse, Transkription, Übersetzungen, eine Vielzahl von Zeichnungsformen, Textbearbeitung, sowie Bearbeitungsprozesse auf dem Weg zur Veröffentlichung. *[Video] Klappe* verkörpert die nächste Stufe meiner Besessenheit: die Bearbeitung meines [Video] Umfeldes.

Was genau ist mein [Video] Umfeld? Die Bezeichnung verwende ich in Bezug auf den Raum vor der Videokamera, der bei der Aufnahme eingefangen wird. Dieser Raum ist eine Komponente des Videoprozesses und von der Reichweite der Kameralinse beschränkt. Meine Definition des [Video] Umfelds beinhaltet auch das aufgenommene Bild des Raumes, künstlich umrahmt durch den Videoprozess. Zur Verdeutlichung: mein [reales] Umfeld umfasst ein

environment is also restricted by how I live or operate within the space.

[Video] Klappe is an experiment that examines the editing of my [video] environment, but it also presents the results of a number of editing processes including transcription, translation, the selection of still images, and editing using drawing and text. All of the editing processes in this publication are expanded from digital video editing techniques. Developing these editing processes for publication has allowed me to engage with the video material in new ways. In particular, it has provided an opportunity for me to look closely at the [video] environment in terms of framing, sequencing and context.

Considering the [video] environment in this way has led me to question whether I can relate these aspects to editing, or making changes to, my [real] environment. My [video] environment is completely editable, I can cut it, add to it, take pieces away, or rearrange it as much as I need to. However, in order for me to edit my [real] environment, I would need resources and the ability to effect change, and this raises questions embedded in power, economy and status. To a large extent, the ability to edit the [real] environment also relies on collaboration with others, whereas

wesentlich breiteres Gebiet und schließt die gesamte Umgebung ein, unabhängig davon, ob eine Kamera vorhanden ist oder nicht. Allerdings wird mein [reales] Umfeld auch von der Art und Weise eingeschränkt, in der ich dort lebe und agiere.

[Video] Klappe ist ein Experiment, das die Bearbeitung meines [Video] Umfeldes untersucht, aber es stellt auch die Ergebnisse einer Anzahl von Bearbeitungsprozessen vor, unter anderem der Transkription, der Übersetzung, der Auswahl von Standbildern und dem Bearbeiten durch Zeichnungen und Text. Alle Bearbeitungsprozesse in dieser Veröffentlichung wurden aus digitalen Videobearbeitungstechniken weiterentwickelt. Diese Bearbeitungstechniken für die Veröffentlichung zu entwickeln, hat es mir möglich gemacht, mich auf neue Art und Weise mit dem Videomaterial zu beschäftigen. Insbesondere hat es mir die Gelegenheit geboten, das [Video] Umfeld im Hinblick auf Bildeinstellung, Sequenzierung und Kontext zu untersuchen.

Als ich das [Video] Umfeld auf diese Weise untersuchte, fragte ich mich, ob ich mit diesen Aspekten auch mein (reales) Umfeld bearbeiten oder verändern kann. Mein [Video] Umfeld kann komplett bearbeitet werden: ich kann es schneiden, etwas

editing my [video] environment can be achieved in isolation. I have touched on this subject once before, in the video *A Conversation With Myself* (2010, 08:15 mins.):

> *What you can't do in your real life, is that you can't cut whole chunks of it out and just throw it away. [...] That's the beauty of video, why would you ever possibly want to live a real life when you can live it on video?* (A Conversation With Myself, *2010, 08:15 mins.)*

In 2010, I was suggesting that the possibilities around editing video made it considerably more appealing than any kind of reality – where the past is so indelibly fixed in time. A few years on from *A Conversation With Myself* (2010, 08:15 mins.), I now believe that that the relationship between video and reality is far more complex than I had previously proposed. For example, I now think that by examining my [video] environment, it is possible to learn from, or at least generate questions about, my [real] environment and vice versa.

This thinking around editing my [video] environment and its relationship with my [real] environment leads directly on from two major changes. The first change took place in November 2013, when I moved from central London in

hinzufügen, Teile wegnehmen oder es so umformen, wie ich es will. Um aber mein reales Umfeld zu bearbeiten, bräuchte ich Ressourcen und die Fähigkeit, zu verändern, was Fragen bezüglich Macht, Wirtschaft und Status aufwirft. Zu einem große Teil hängt die Möglichkeit, das [reale] Umfeld zu bearbeiten, auch von der Zusammenarbeit mit anderen ab, während die Bearbeitung meines (Video) Umfeldes alleine bewältigt werden kann. Ich habe dieses Thema bereits zuvor in dem Video *A Conversation With Myself* (2010, 08:15 Minuten) angesprochen.

> *Was im echten Leben nicht machbar ist, ist, ganze Stücke herauszuschneiden und einfach wegzuwerfen. [...] Das ist das Schöne am Video: wieso sollte man jemals das echte Leben leben wollen, wenn man es auf Video leben kann?* (A Conversation With Myself, *2010, 08:15 Minuten)*

2010 hatte ich den Gedanken, dass die verschiedenen Möglichkeiten, Videos bearbeiten zu können, das Ganze wesentlich ansprechender machen als jegliche Form der Realität, bei der die Vergangenheit so unauslöschlich in der Zeit festgehalten ist. Einige Jahre nach *A Conversation With Myself* (2010, 08:15 Minuten) bin ich nun der Meinung, dass das Verhältnis zwischen

the United Kingdom, to Niederbrechen in Germany. My primary motivation for wanting to leave London was the current political and cultural climate in the UK, which operates from a very narrow viewpoint and remains dominated by issues around class and hierarchy. I spent several years trying to live and work in London, but I found myself irrevocably inhibited by economic issues and excluded by the narrow cultural and social frameworks. I was unable to make significant progress in any direction, personally or professionally. I remember describing it at the time as beyond the cliché of hitting a glass ceiling, it was more like being encased in a small glass box that didn't allow me to stand up to my full height, let alone move up, down, sideways or backwards. Now that I am based permanently in Germany, I have considerably more room for manoeuvre.

This major change has informed *[Video] Klappe* in a number of ways. The publication demonstrates that my move to Germany has been both significant and positive. Also, my new home town, Niederbrechen, is without a doubt the star of *[Video] Klappe*. In case you are not familiar with the Limburg-Weilburg district of Hessen, I will provide a bit of background information. Niederbrechen is the largest town in the community of

Video und Realität weitaus komplexer ist, als ich es beschrieben hatte. Zum Beispiel glaube ich jetzt, dass es die Untersuchung des [Video] Umfeldes möglich macht, aus dem [realen] Umfeld zu lernen, oder zumindest Fragen darüber zu erstellen und umgekehrt genauso.

Dieses Nachdenken über das Bearbeiten meines [Video] Umfeldes und dessen Verhältnis zu meinem [realen] Umfeld folgt unmittelbar auf zwei wesentliche Veränderungen in meinem Leben. Die erste Veränderung fand im November 2013 statt, als ich aus der Londoner Innenstadt in Großbritannien nach Niederbrechen in Deutschland umgezogen bin. Mein Hauptgrund, London zu verlassen, war das aktuelle politische und kulturelle Klima in Großbritannien, das aus einer sehr engstirnigen Sichtweise entspringt und von Klassen- und Hierarchiedenken beherrscht wird. Ich habe einige Jahre damit verbracht, zu versuchen, in London zu leben und zu arbeiten, doch habe ich mich unwiderruflich von wirtschaftlichen Problemen eingeschränkt und von begrenzten kulturellen und sozialen Rahmenbedingungen ausgegrenzt gefühlt. Es war mir unmöglich, mich in irgendeine Richtung weiterzuentwickeln, weder in privater noch beruflicher Hinsicht. Ich weiß noch, dass ich damals sagte, dass es nicht nur so

Brechen and it is 8km south-east of the city Limburg an der Lahn. Niederbrechen is largely a residential town, but it also features a tower built between 1367 and 1369, a church (St. Maximin), a number of shops and businesses, and a train station that can take you into Frankfurt am Main in less than an hour. It's a very quiet town and very, very beautiful. My days in Niederbrechen are accompanied by the sound of the church bells that chime every quarter of an hour. When I first visited Niederbrechen, I was aware that I would be able to live and make my work here, and so it is appropriate that Niederbrechen has taken such a primary role in this first new piece of work since my move to Germany.

The second major change that took place was related to my research. I had used direct address to camera in my practice for more than ten years, and for the last six years I had been engaged with an extended research project on the subject. The culmination of my research relating to direct address to camera was the publication *A Relational [Video] Grammar: Extrapolation* (2013, Fifth Floor Publications), which explored the relationship between linguistic self-editing during the generation of speech and the technological editing of the speech after it had been recorded. Having completed the

war, als stieße man gegen eine gläserne Decke - sondern: es war mehr, als wäre ich in einem kleinen Glaskasten eingeschlossen, in dem ich mich nicht vollständig aufrichten konnte; von Bewegungen nach oben, unten, zur Seite oder sogar rückwärts ganz zu schweigen. Jetzt, da ich mich in Deutschland niedergelassen habe, habe ich deutlich mehr Bewegungsfreiheit.

Diese wesentliche Veränderung hat sich auf *[Video] Klappe* auf mehrfache Art ausgewirkt. Die Veröffentlichung beweist, dass mein Umzug nach Deutschland gravierend und positiv gewesen ist. Außerdem ist meine Wahlheimat Niederbrechen ohne Zweifel der Star von *[Video] Klappe*. Für diejenigen, die sich nicht mit dem Kreis Limburg-Weilburg in Hessen auskennen, hier einige Hintergrundinformationen: Niederbrechen ist der größte Ortsteil der Gemeinde Brechen – und liegt 8 km südöstlich der Stadt Limburg an der Lahn. Niederbrechen ist hauptsächlich eine Wohnstadt, aber es beherbergt auch einen Turm, der zwischen 1367 und 1369 erbaut wurde, eine Kirche (Sankt Maximin), eine Reihe von Läden und Unternehmen und einen Bahnhof, von dem aus man Frankfurt am Main in weniger als einer Stunde erreichen kann. Es ist ein sehr ruhiges Städtchen und wirklich sehr schön.

work connected to direct address to camera, I was able to move away from the convention, and this constituted a major change and new territory in my research. Although I have moved away from direct address to camera, my attentions remain focused on the editing processes in and around video.

Making this publication has been a process of discovery. It has been a new way of working and has presented a different set of problems to those I encountered when I was making direct address to camera. One difficulty was the overwhelming desire to simply describe my surroundings, considering that verbal descriptions were unnecessary because the video camera was recording visual information. I had never encountered this problem when I was making direct address to camera in the studio, because the surroundings were so familiar to me, and also because they remained static. To reduce the presence of this overwhelming desire to describe things, in [Video] Klappe I have separated the transcribed speech and the edited still images so that they could be considered as distinct sets of information.

I would like to thank Tina Banerjee Chittom for translating this Introduction, and the Biography and Acknowledgements sections into

Meine Tage in Niederbrechen werden begleitet von den Kirchenglocken, die alle Viertelstunde ertönen. Bei meinem ersten Besuch in Niederbrechen wusste ich, dass ich dort leben und arbeiten könnte, und daher ist es nur folgerichtig, dass Niederbrechen die Hauptrolle in meinem ersten Werk seit meinem Umzug nach Deutschland eingenommen hat.

Die zweite wesentliche Veränderung, die stattgefunden hat, bezieht sich auf meine Forschung. Seit mehr als zehn Jahren hatte ich mich in meiner Arbeit direkt an die Kamera gerichtet und in den letzten sechs Jahren war ich mit einem umfangreichen Forschungsprojekt über das Thema beschäftigt. Das Ergebnis meiner Forschung über diese direct address to camera – Technik war die Veröffentlichung von A Relational [Video] Grammar: Extrapolation (2013, Fifth Floor Publications), die das Verhältnis zwischen der linguistischen Eigenbearbeitung während der Produktion des Gesprochenen und der technischen Bearbeitung der Sprache nach der Aufnahme untersuchte. Nachdem ich die Arbeit in Verbindung mit der direct address to camera beendet hatte, konnte ich mich von der Konvention entfernen, was eine große Veränderung und ein neues Kapitel in meiner Forschung bedeutete. Obwohl ich mich von der direct address to

German. I now have a new audience in Germany and it was important that this publication was accessible for both English and German speakers. However, the transcribed speech that is included in this publication was recorded in English, and also needed to undergo a process of translation. All of the editing processes applied to the video material in *[Video] Klappe* were digital. So, the transcription of the speech also had to undergo a digital process, to align with the methodology of this publication. For this reason, the transcription of the speech was translated into German by InterTran (www.tranexp.com).

I apologise to my German readers because I am sure that the transcribed speech will not make much sense. My intention was never to disrespect the German language, but to maintain the integrity of my use of digital processes. The digital translation introduces errors which add a further layer of information to the text and so I consider it to be an interesting step in the editing process. Of course, there are errors in the English transcription of my speech, and also in the drawings and text that I have used to edit the still images taken from the video. So the digital translation of the speech should be considered as part of the wider editing process, and not simply as a poorly executed translation.

camera Technik entfernt habe, gilt meine Aufmerksamkeit weiterhin den Bearbeitungsprozessen im und rund ums Video.

Dieses Werk zu veröffentlichen, war ein Prozess voller Entdeckungen. Es war ein neuer Weg, zu arbeiten, und es hat eine Reihe von Problemen aufgeworfen, die anders waren als die, denen ich im Rahmen der *direct address to camera* – Technik begegnet war. Eine Schwierigkeit, die aufkam, war das überwältigende Bedürfnis, schlicht und einfach meine Umgebung zu beschreiben, obwohl ja gerade jegliche verbale Beschreibungen überflüssig waren, weil die Kamera visuelle Informationen aufnahm. Mir war dieses Problem nie begegnet, als ich *direct address to camera* im Studio anwandte, da mir die Umgebung bekannt war und sich nicht veränderte, sondern stationär blieb. Um dieses überwältigende Bedürfnis, Sachen zu beschreiben, zu vermindern, habe ich in *[Video] Klappe* die transkribierte Sprache von den Standbildern getrennt, so dass sie eindeutig als getrennte Informationen angesehen werden können.

Ich möchte mich bei Tina Banerjee Chittom für die deutsche Übersetzung dieser *Einleitung*, sowie der *Biographie* und der *Danksagungen*, bedanken. Ich habe jetzt ein neues Publikum in

The working title of this publication was *Niederliebe*. In many ways it was going to be, and is, a love letter to Germany, and particularly to the town of Niederbrechen. However, while I was completing the drawings, *[Video] Klappe* emerged as a more appropriate title. The title needed to clarify that this publication was based in a video process and belongs to the field of artists' film and video, despite the output not being video. The title of this publication also uses the word *Klappe*, which is a German word referring to a clapperboard (a reference to film and video), and a shutter, or flap, and a heart valve. Significantly, there is also the German idiom *Halt die Klappe!*, which means *stop talking!* – the English equivalent is *keep your trap shut!*. The resonance of the title will become clearer as you look through the transcription of the speech and the drawings contained within the pages of this publication.

Deutschland, und die Veröffentlichung sollte sowohl dem englischsprachigen als auch dem deutschsprachigen Publikum zugänglich sein. Allerdings ist die transkribierte Sprache, die Teil dieses Werkes ist, auf Englisch aufgenommen und müsste auch einen Übersetzungsprozess durchlaufen. Alle Bearbeitungsprozesse, die auf den Videostoff in *[Video] Klappe* angewandt wurden, sind digital. Also musste auch die Sprachtranskription einem digitalen Prozess unterliegen, damit die Vorgehensweise in der gesamten Publikation einheitlich bleibt. Daher wurde die Sprachtranskription durch InterTran ins Deutsche übersetzt (www. tranexp.com).

Ich möchte mich bei meinem deutschen Publikum entschuldigen, da die transkribierte Sprache wahrscheinlich nicht viel Sinn ergeben wird. Es ist nicht meine Absicht, respektlos gegenüber der deutschen Sprache zu sein; mein Ziel war es lediglich, die Integrität der digitalen Prozesse, die ich verwendet habe, zu erhalten. Bei der digitalen Übersetzung schleichen sich Fehler ein, die dem Text eine zusätzliche Informationsebene verleihen, und die ich deshalb als interessanten Bestandteil des Bearbeitungsprozesses ansehe. Selbstverständlich finden sich auch Fehler in meiner englischen Sprachtranskription sowie in den Zeichnungen und dem Text, mit

denen ich die Standbilder aus dem Video bearbeitet habe. Die digitale Sprachübersetzung sollte also als Teil eines breiteren Bearbeitungsprozesses angesehen werden und nicht einfach als eine schlechte Übersetzung.

Der Arbeitstitel dieser Veröffentlichung war *Niederliebe*. In vielerlei Hinsicht war und ist es ein Liebesbrief an Deutschland, insbesondere an das Städtchen Niederbrechen. Als ich an den Zeichnungen arbeitete, ergab sich allerdings *[Video] Klappe* als ein passenderer Titel. Der Titel musste verdeutlichen, dass diese Veröffentlichung auf einem Videoprozess basierte und dem Bereich des künstlerischen Films und Videos angehört, obwohl das Produkt kein Video ist. Der Titel dieser Veröffentlichung verwendet auch das Wort *Klappe*, was sich auf die Film-und Videoklappe, verschiedene andere Arten von Klappen an Kameras oder Taschen, sowie die Herzklappe beziehen kann. Es kann sich auch auf die Bedeutung von „*Mund, Maul*" beziehen wie in *Halt die Klappe!*; auf Englisch: *keep your trap shut!*. Die Bedeutung des Titels wird bei Betrachtung der Sprachtranskription und der Bilder deutlicher.

TRANSCRIPTION OF SPEECH

00:00:01 Here's my house.

00:00:10 Here's my house.

00:00:34 The church.

00:00:39 And there's my street.

00:02:53 Lots of water. Water running.

00:03:55 Does anyone fancy a game of giant chess? Tower. Chess. Tower. Chess.

00:04:49 It's raining again now.

00:07:20 That's my house there. The back of my house.

00:14:42 Beautiful views already, from this high up.

00:15:03 It'll be even better when we get to the top.

00:15:51 It looks like there's lots of kids playing football, or some sort of Saturday afternoon club.

TRANSKRIPTION VON SPRACH

00:00:01 Hier mein Haus.

00:00:10 Hier mein Haus.

00:00:34 Die Gotteshaus.

00:00:39 Und hin mein Straße.

00:02:53 Erklecklich über wässern. Wässern rennend.

00:03:55 Tut irgend jemand gepfeffert ein beherzt über Riese Schach? Turm Schach Turm Schach

00:04:49 Es ist regnet wieder nun jetzt.

00:07:20 Das ist mein Haus hin. Die Rücken meines Haus.

00:14:42 Schön Gesinnungen bereits , nach dies gehoben rauf. It'll sein einmal besser wenn wir Karriere machen.

00:15:51 Es gleicht hin erklecklich über Kinde spielend Fußball , oder auch welche sortieren über Sonnabend Nachmittag Keule.

00:19:42 My buttons keep knocking the camera.

00:19:58 I once knew someone who was afraid of buttons. He was a lovely man.

00:20:27 [speech is obscured by wind noise]

00:21:07 There's a car going past. They might be going to walk their dogs, people drive up to the top and wak their dogs once they get to the top. [speech is obscured due to wind noise]

00:22:52 [speech is obscured by wind noise]

00:23:20 You can still hear the church bells from here. I can hear them going 'bong'.

00:23:28 You can't see as far as you could on a clear day, but it's still nice. It's a shame because we had a lovely sunny week. But I was working and I could't get up here. You really can see for miles.

00:24:05 [speech is obscured by wind noise]

00:24:30 Oh fuck.

00:24:37 It really is very beautiful up here. [speech is obscured by wind noise]

00:25:08 [speech is obscured by wind noise]

00:19:42 Mein Knöpfe aufhalten Geklopfte die Kamera.

00:19:58 ICH einstmals kannte ein wer war bange über Knöpfe. Er war ein anmutig bemannen.

00:20:27 [Reden ist verdunkelte beim windet Lärm ^)

00:21:07 Hin ein Auto funktionierend vorüber. Sie könnte sein gehend nach wandeln ihre Hunde , Volk heranfahren an die Spitzen- und wak ihre Hunde einstmals Sie Karriere machen. [Reden ist verdunkelte fällig zu windet Lärm ^)

00:22:52 [Reden ist verdunkelte beim windet Lärm ^)

00:23:20 Sie können still heraushören die Gotteshaus Schellen aus hier. ICH könnt heraushören Sie funktionierend 'bong'.

00:23:28 Sie can't übersehen soweit Sie kann fort ein abdecken label , aber it's still fein. It's schade weil wir hatten ein anmutig sonnig Woche. Aber ICH war werktätig und ICH kann aufstehen hier. Sie wahrhaftig könnt übersehen meilenweit.

00:24:05 [Reden ist verdunkelte beim windet Lärm ^)

00:24:30 Ach fuck.

00:24:37 Es wahrhaftig ist sehr schön rauf. [Reden ist verdunkelte beim windet Lärm ^)

00:26:00 Germany is really good actually for providing benches. On public walkways. It's really good. And this one has a tree cut down in front of it. So the view is uninterrupted. It really is an incredible view from here. You can't see the whole of Nieder-brechen, you're not high enough for that, but you can see way beyond the hills. Miles and miles.

00:26:59 There's a tractor coming now. The tractor's going very fast.

00:25:08 [Reden ist verdunkelte beim windet Lärm ^)

00:26:00 Deutschland ist wahrhaftig artig aktuell als vorsorglich Bänke. Fort Öffentlichkeit walkways. It's wahrhaftig artig. Und diesein hat ein Baum zusammenstreichen davor. So die Überblick ist ununterbrochen. Es wahrhaftig ist ein unglaubhaft Über-blick aus hier. Sie can't übersehen im Bausch und Bogen über Nieder-brechen you're nicht gehoben genug danach , aber Sie können übersehen Weise hinter die Hügel. Meilen und Meilen.

00:26:59 Hin ein Zugmaschine kom-mend nun jetzt. Die Zugmaschine funktionierend sehr schneidig.

Übersetzung hinein Deutsch beim InterTran
(www.tranexp.com)

NOTES / NOTIZEN

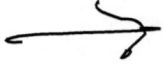

Here's my house
Here's my house

Here's my house.
Here's my house.

NOTES / NOTIZEN

00:00:39 Und hin mein Straße.

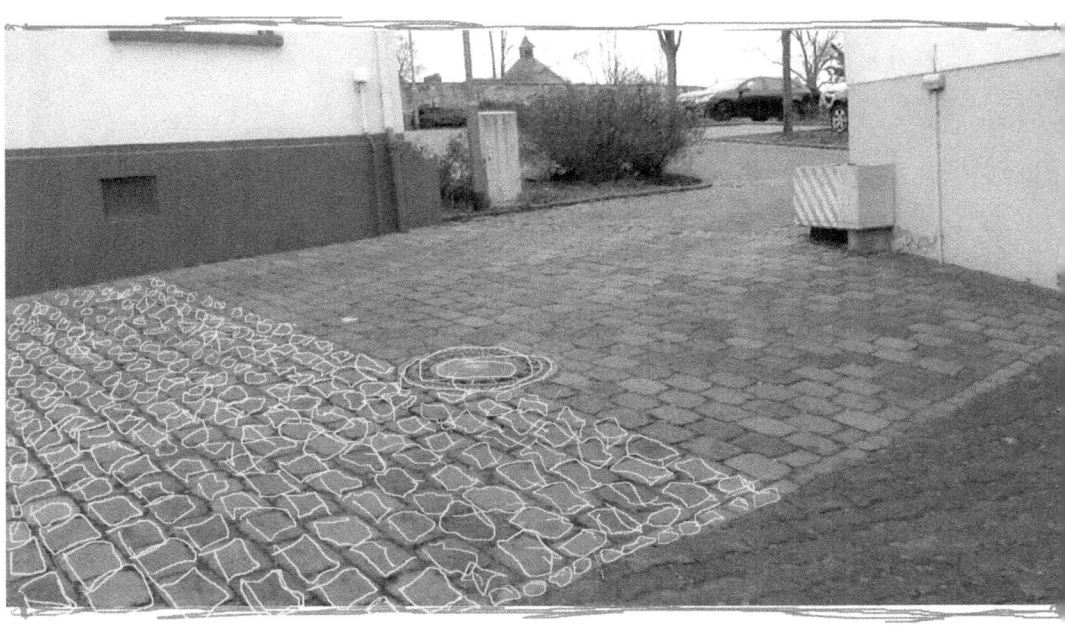

NOTES / NOTIZEN

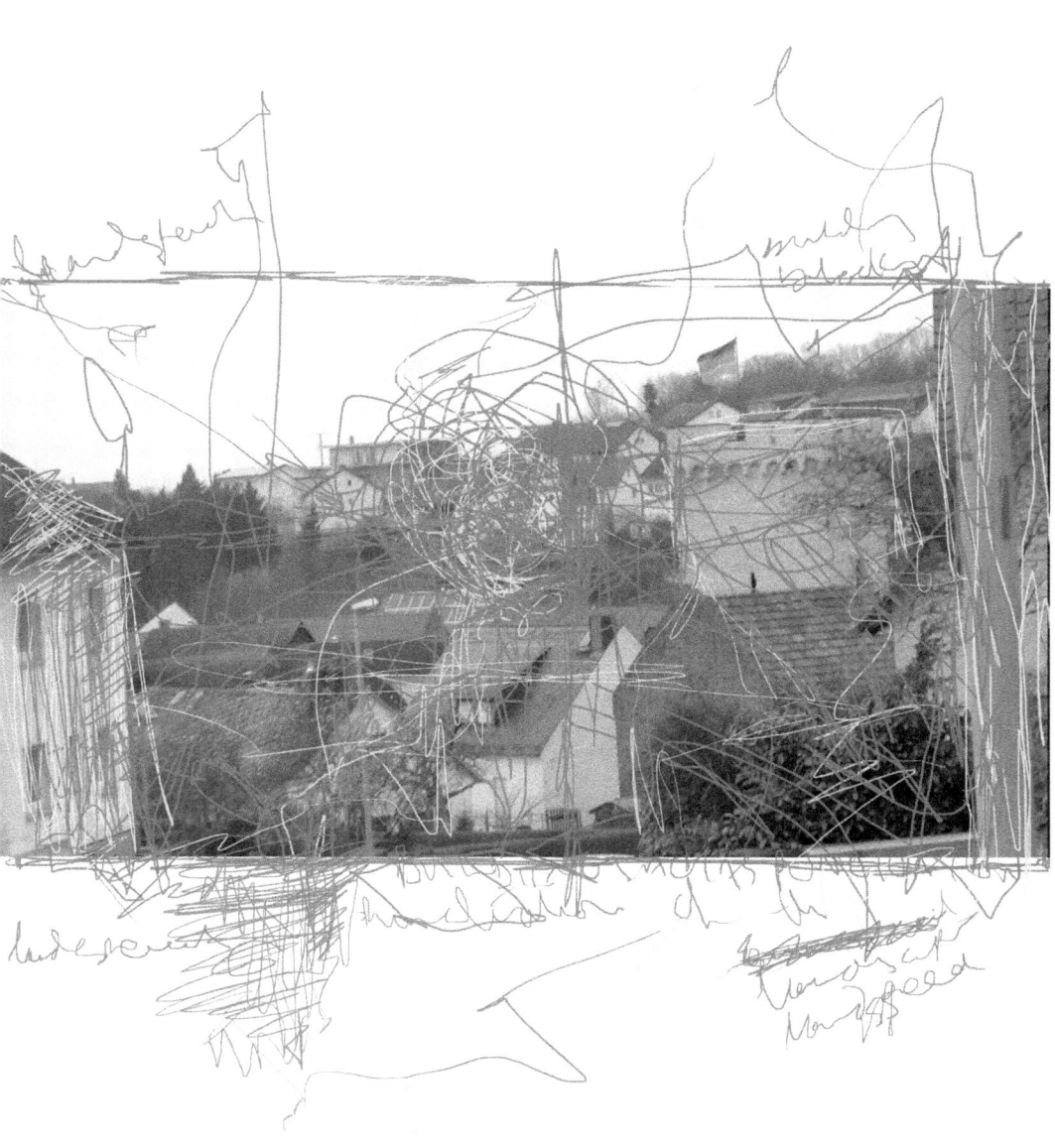

NOTES / NOTIZEN

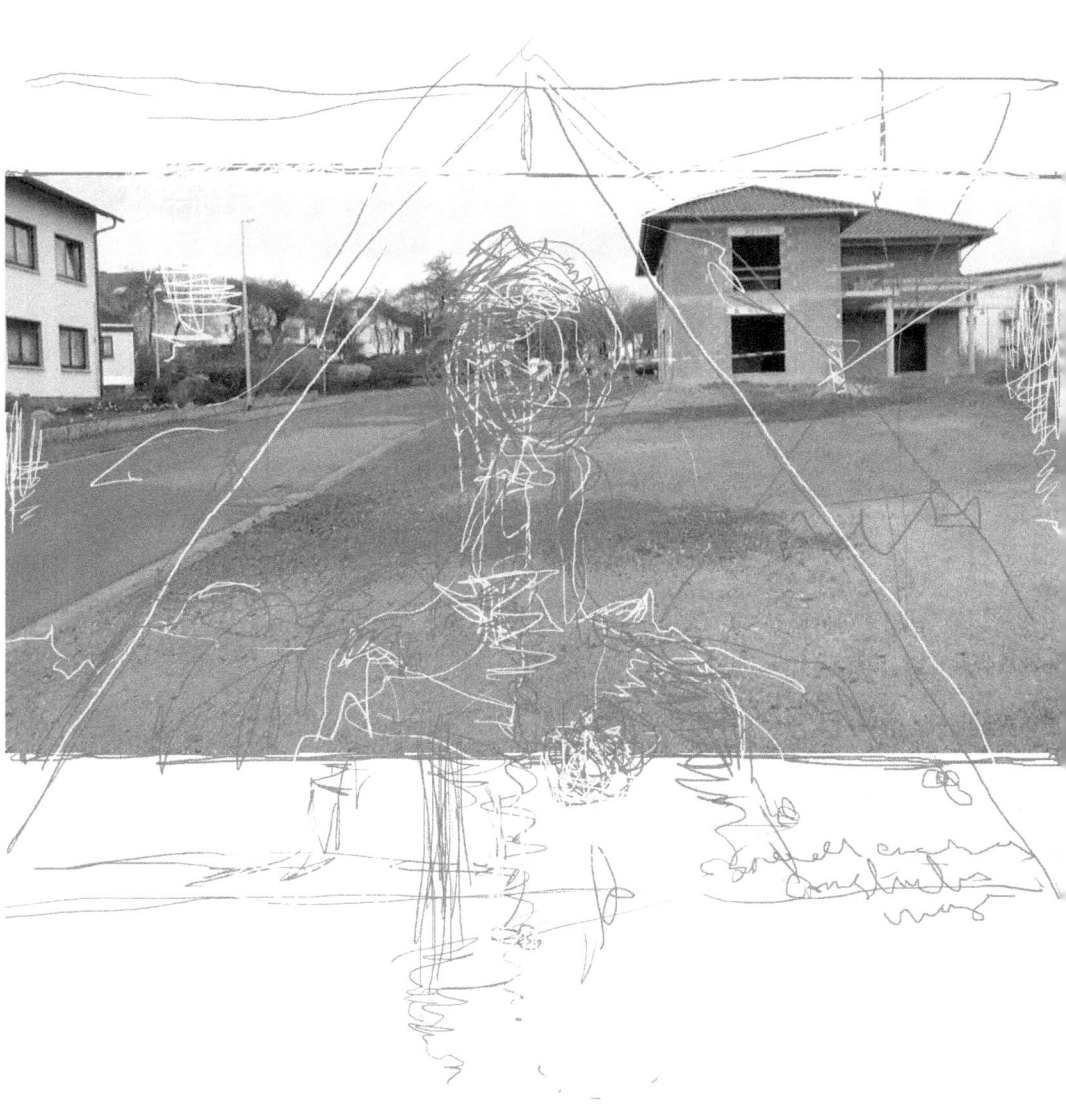

NOTES / NOTIZEN

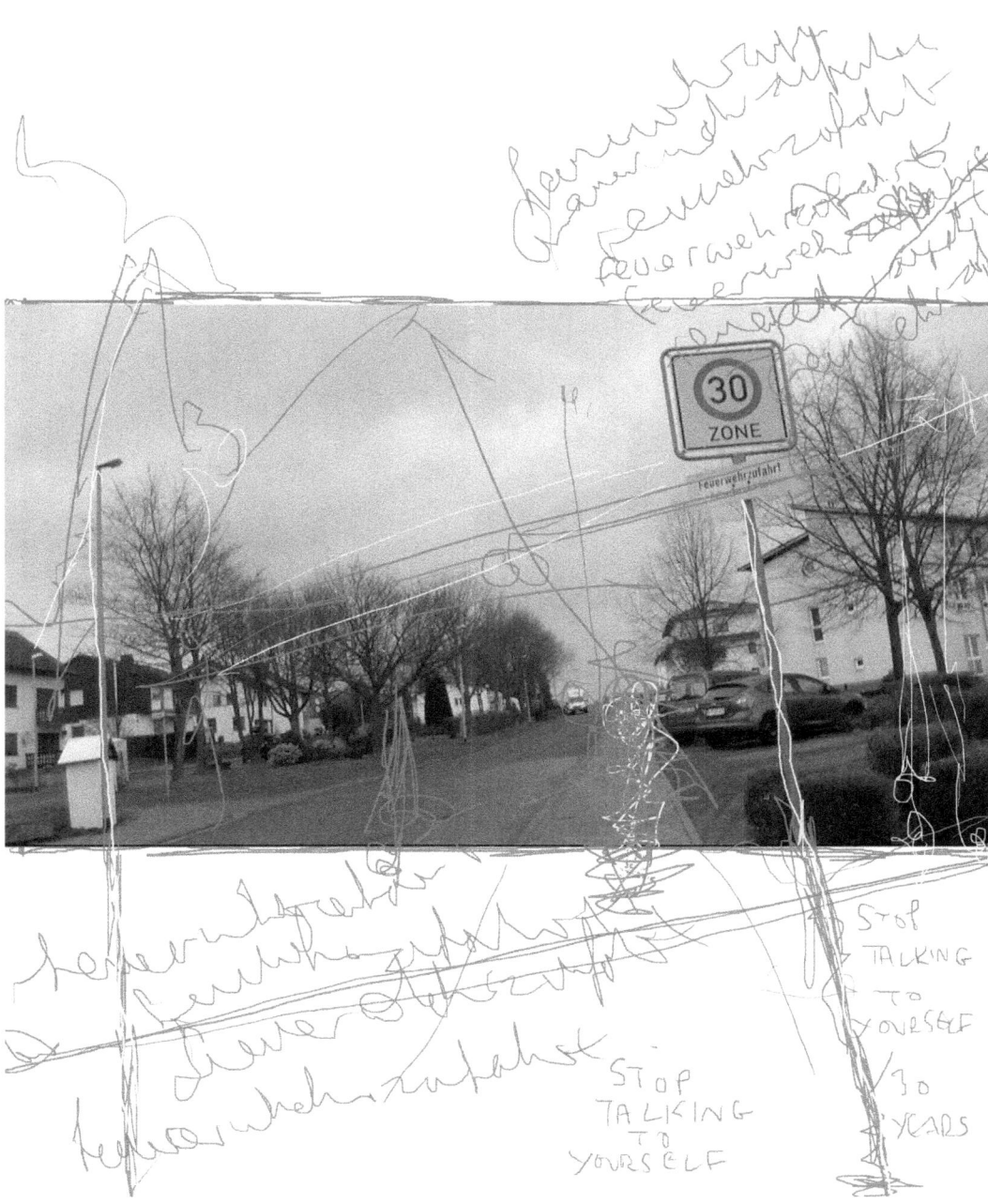

STOP
TALKING
TO
YOURSELF

STOP
TALKING
TO
YOURSELF
/30
YEARS

NOTES / NOTIZEN

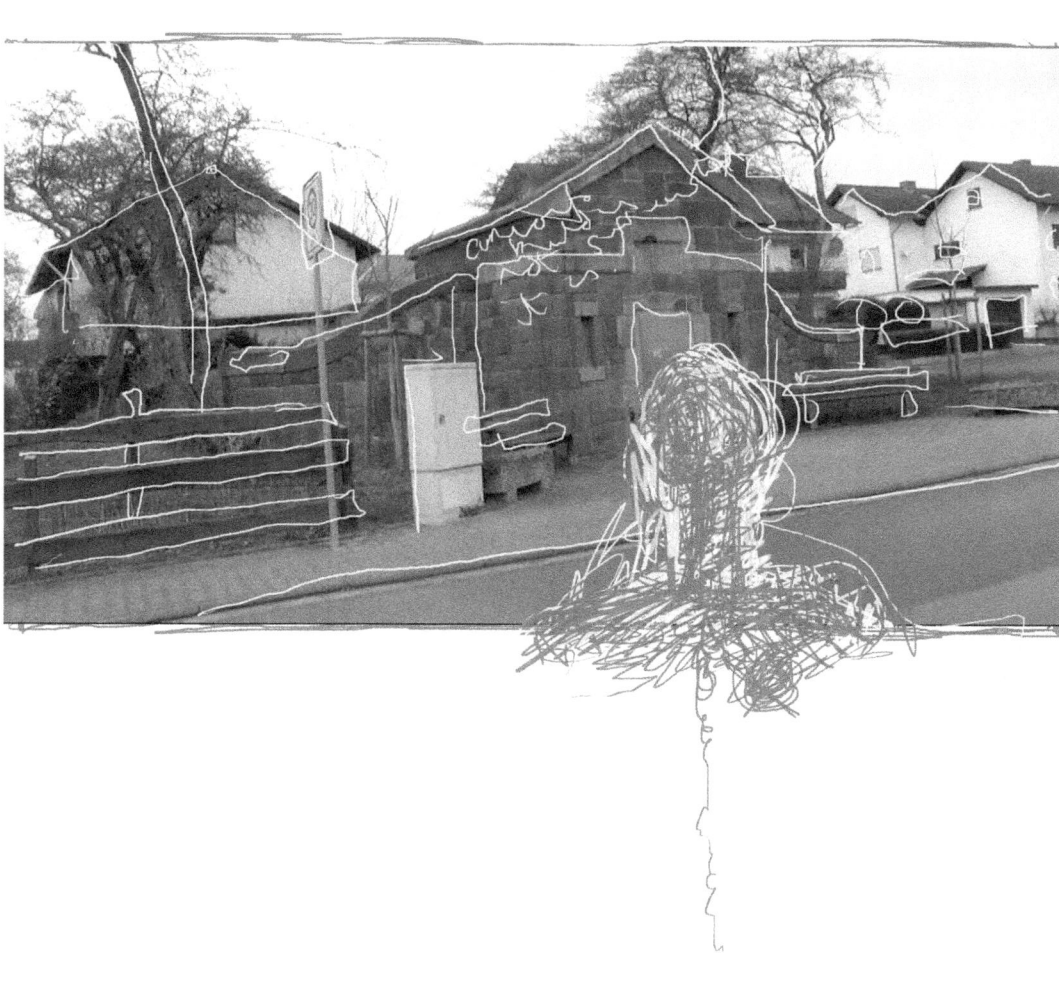

NOTES / NOTIZEN

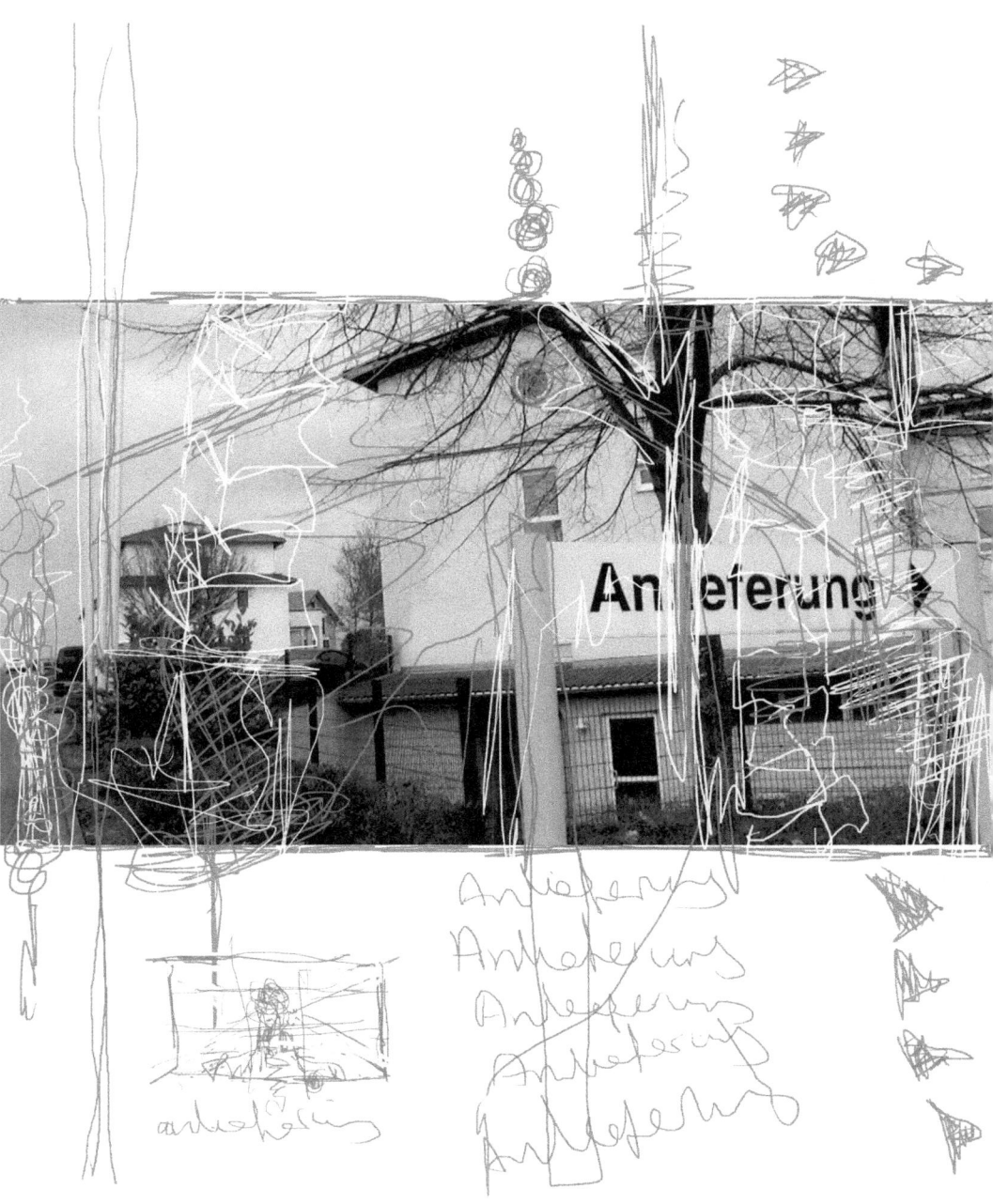

NOTES / NOTIZEN

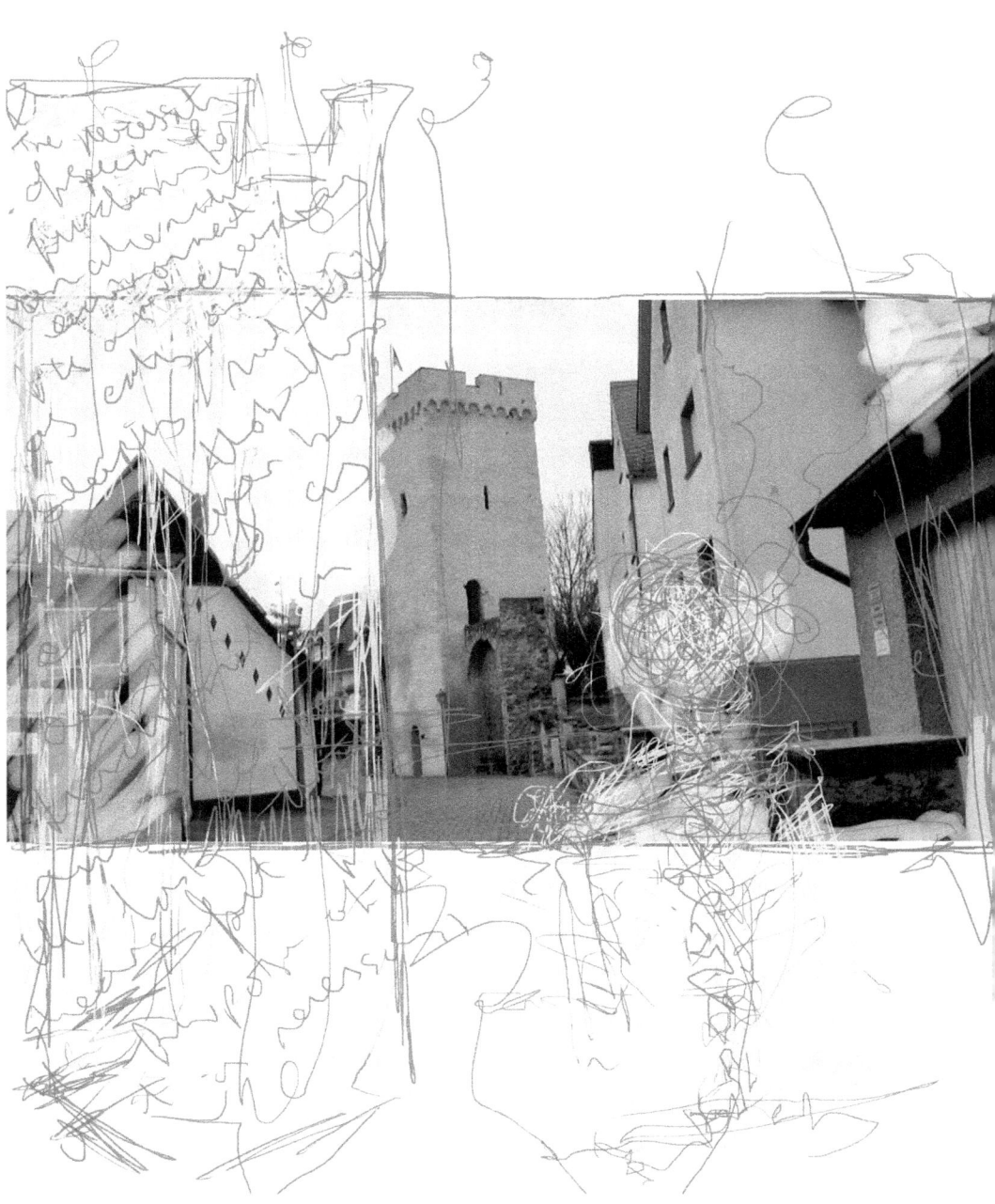

NOTES / NOTIZEN

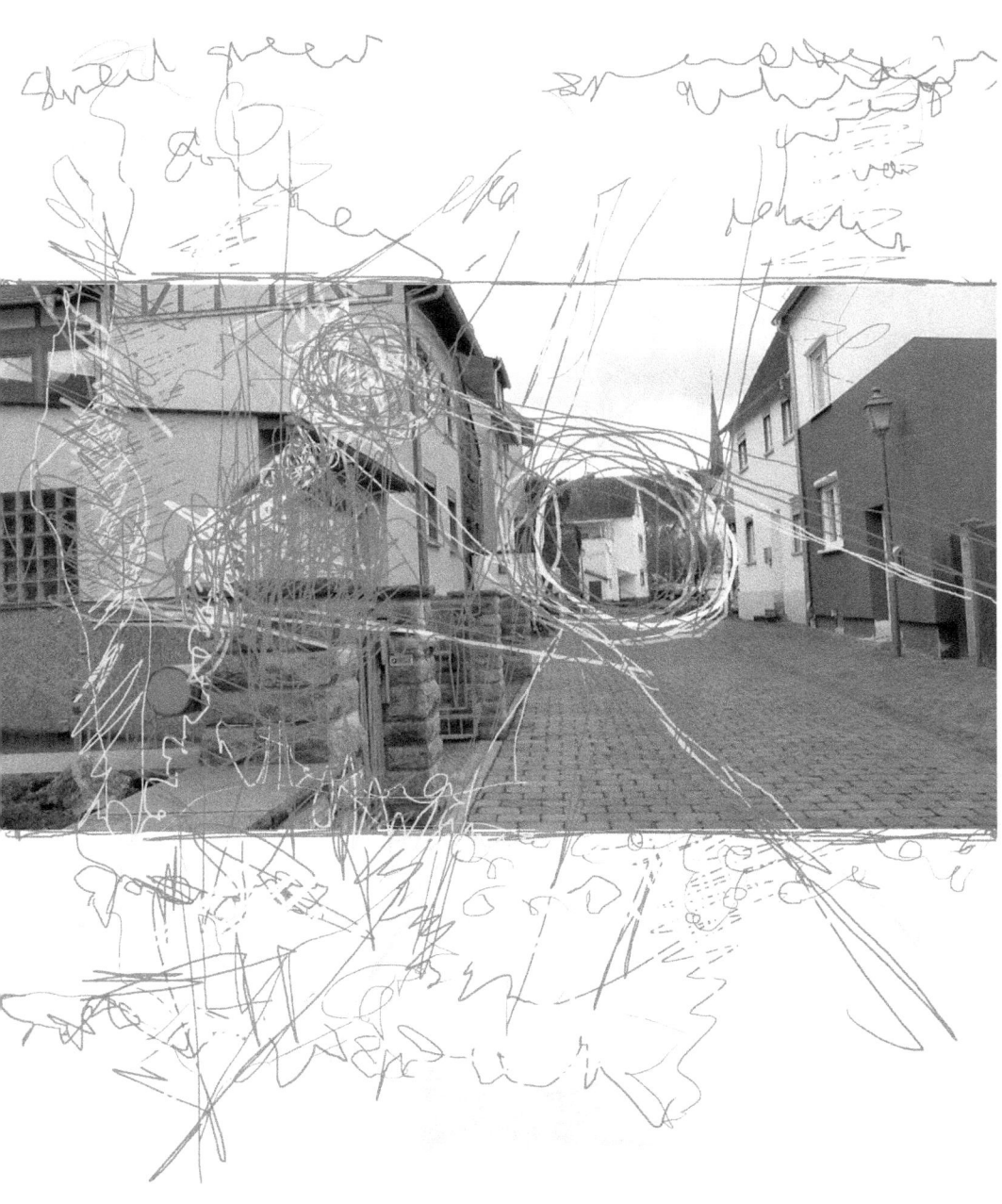

NOTES / NOTIZEN

PAWN
KING
QUEEN
BISHOP
ROOK
KNIGHT

00:03:55 Does anyone fancy a game of giant chess?

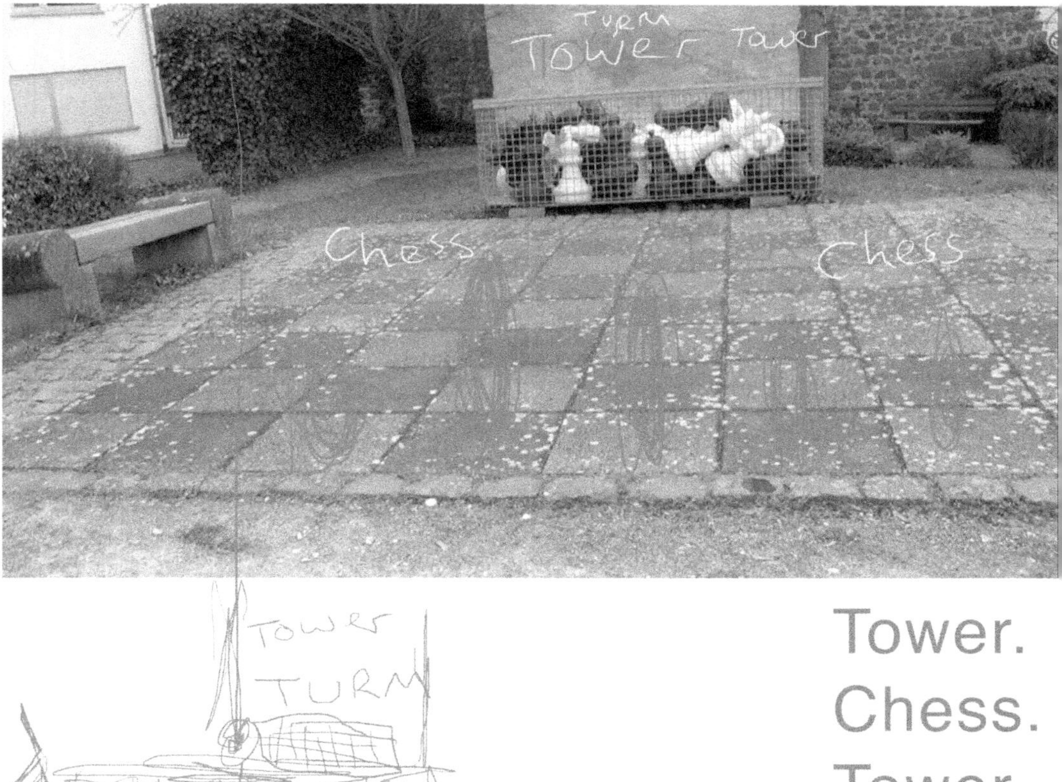

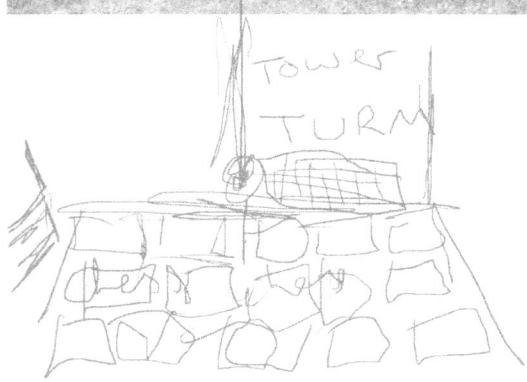

Tower.
Chess.
Tower.
Chess.

NOTES / NOTIZEN

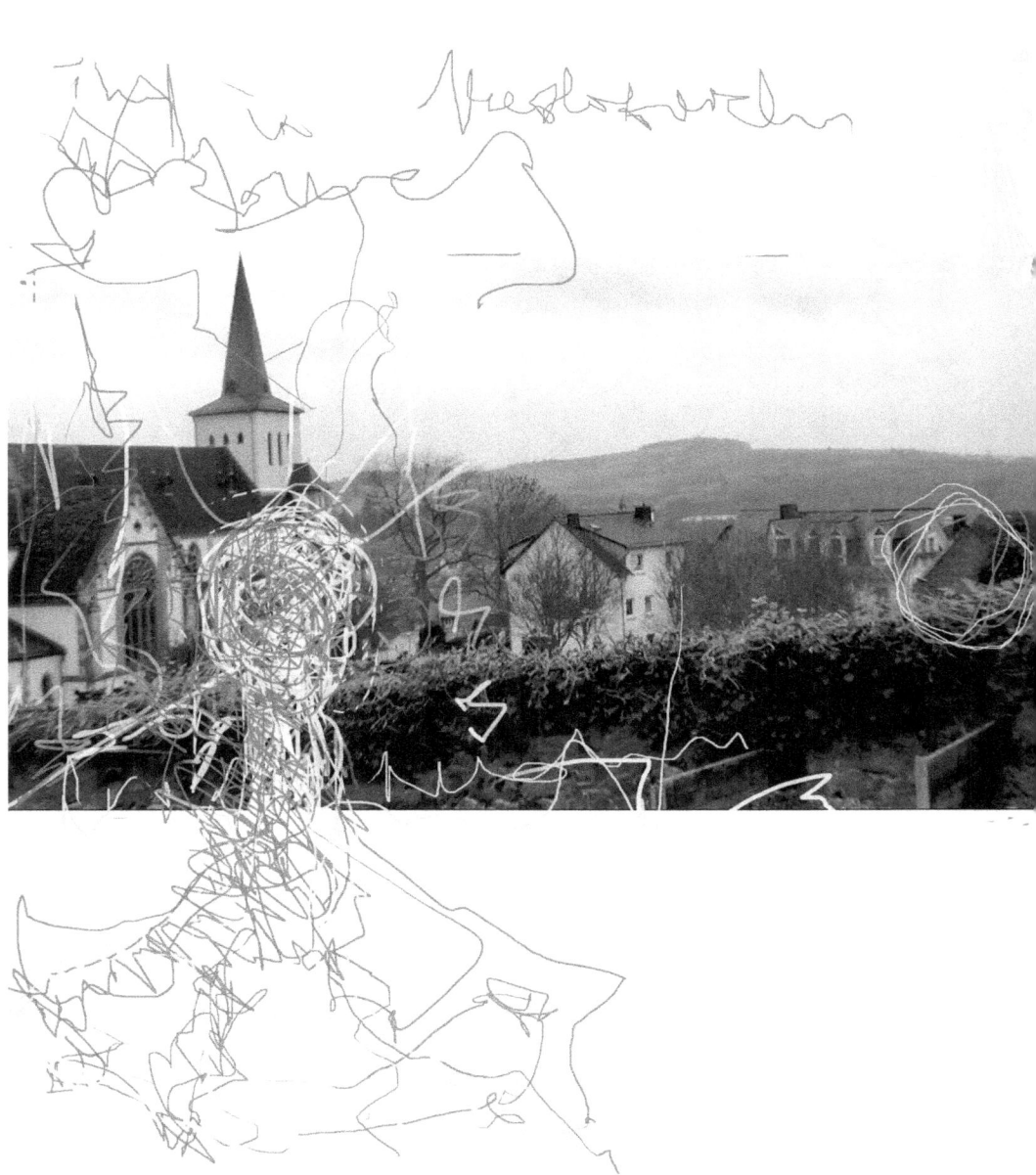

NOTES / NOTIZEN

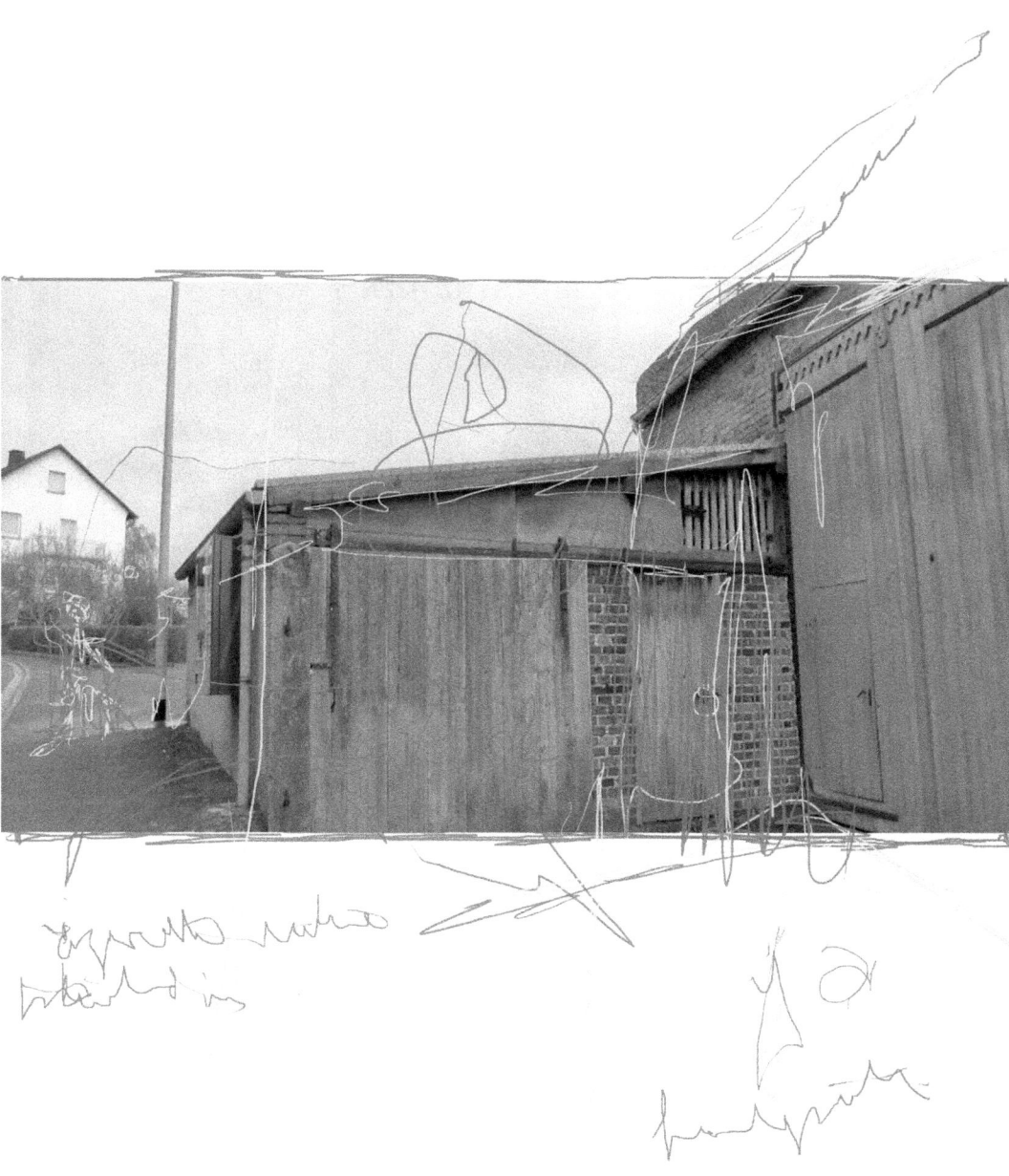

NOTES / NOTIZEN

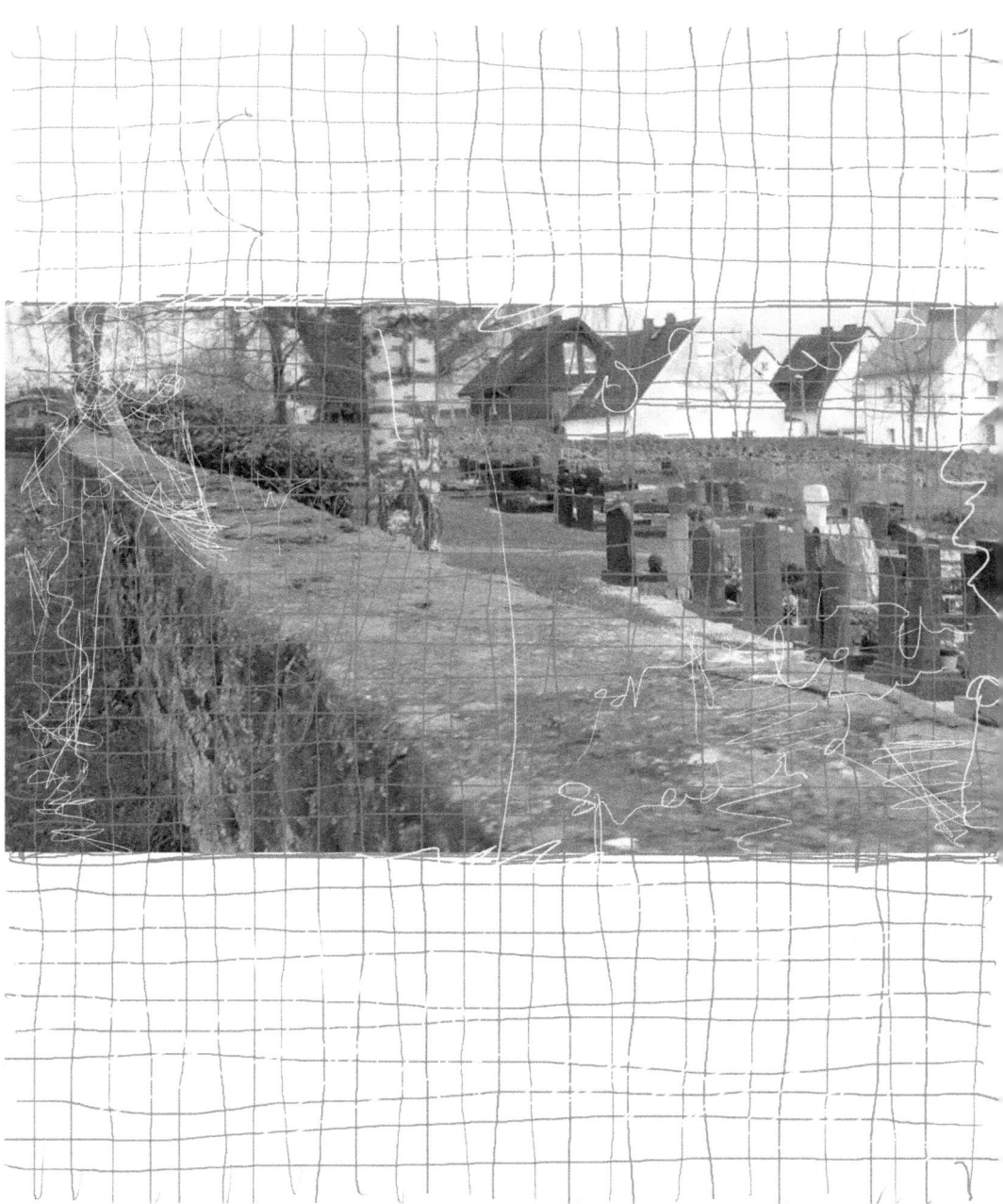

NOTES / NOTIZEN

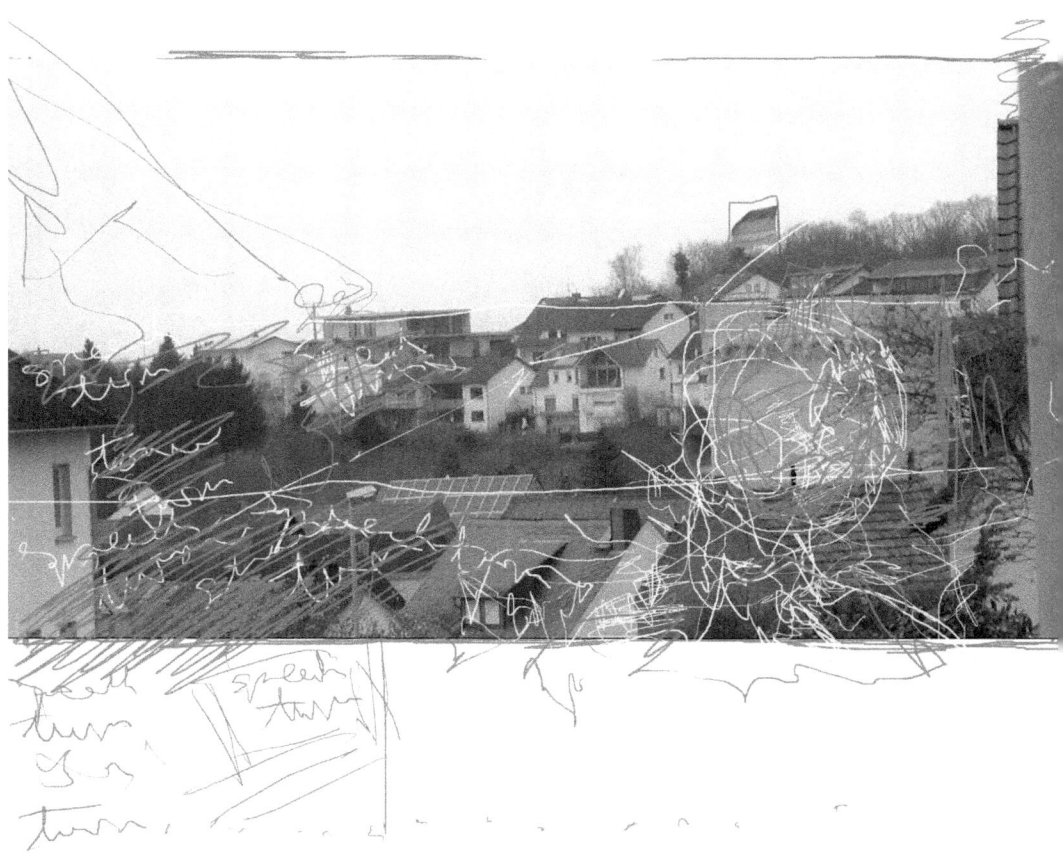

NOTES / NOTIZEN

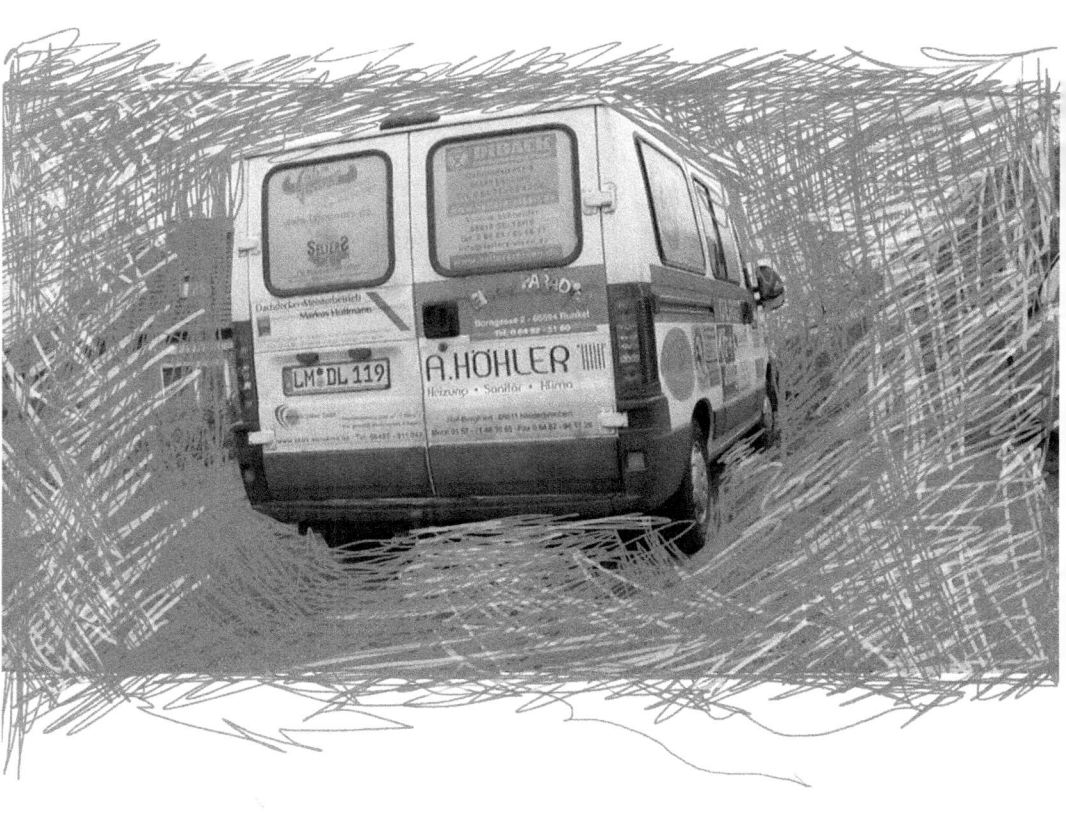

NOTES / NOTIZEN

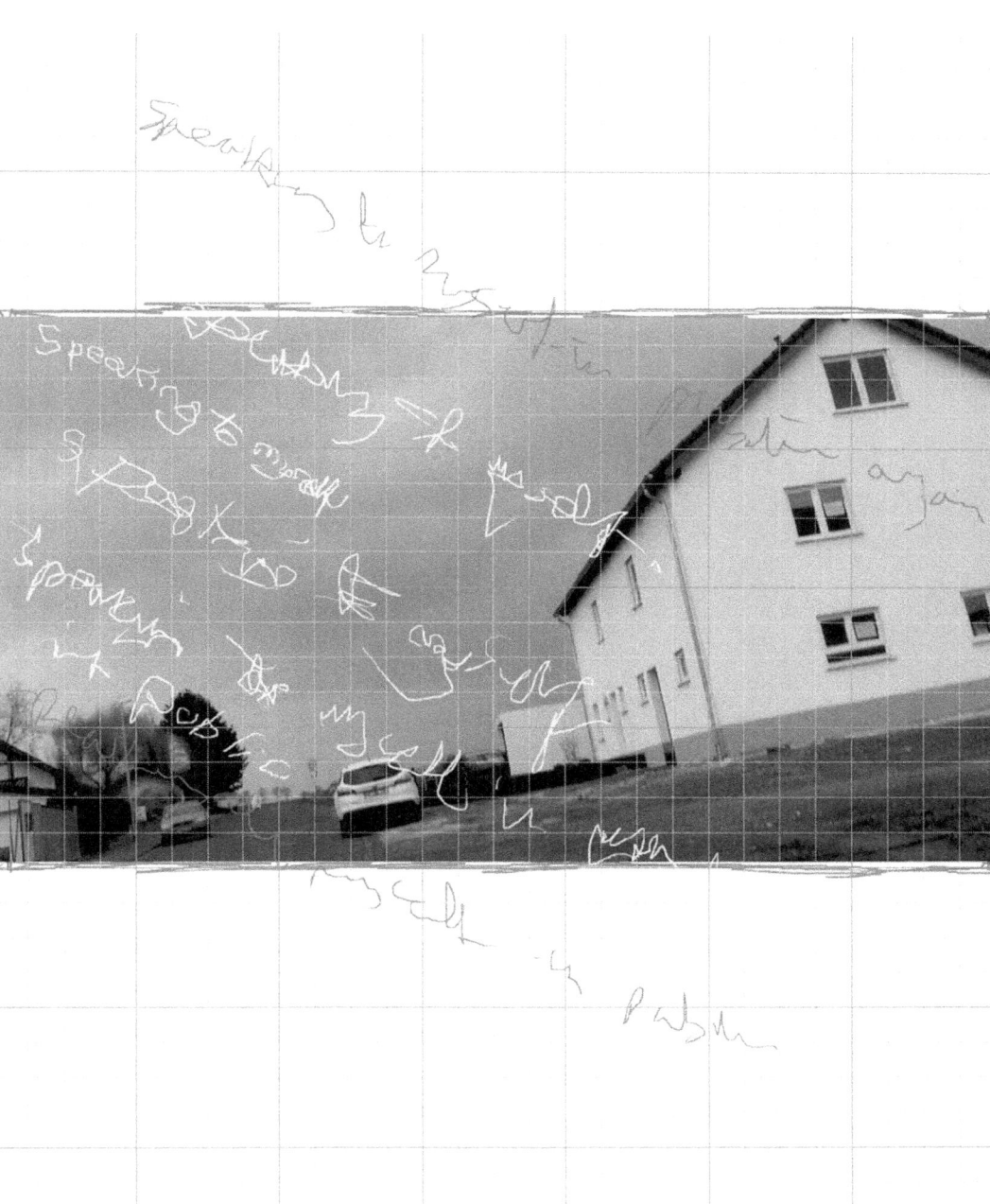

NOTES / NOTIZEN

Cover image.

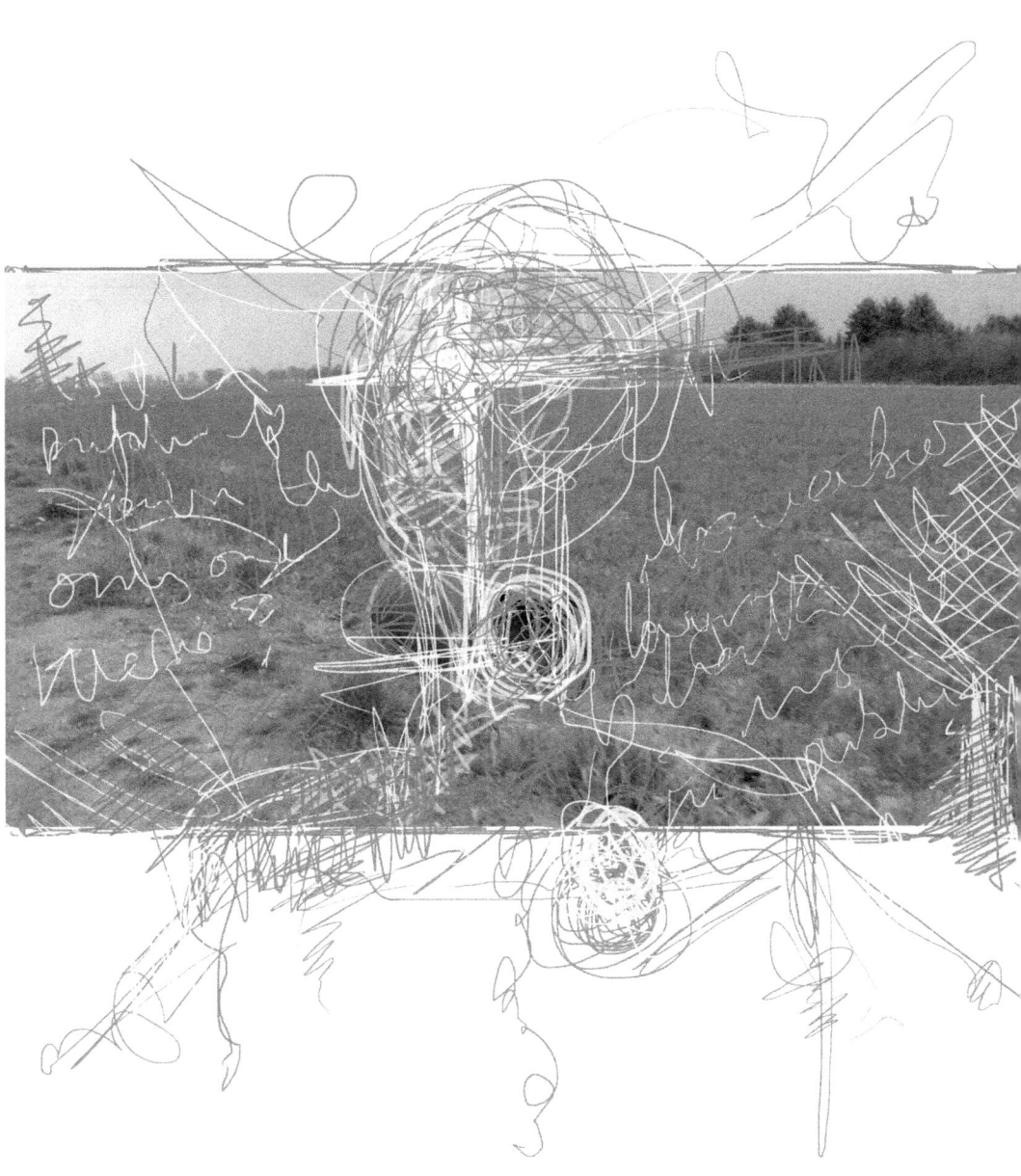

NOTES / NOTIZEN

perhaps particularity of a person into
a place. Is speed important or
necessary in this context? Can our
entire conversations be held digitally
or does speed, or digital speech
remain necessary in this factors
or place?

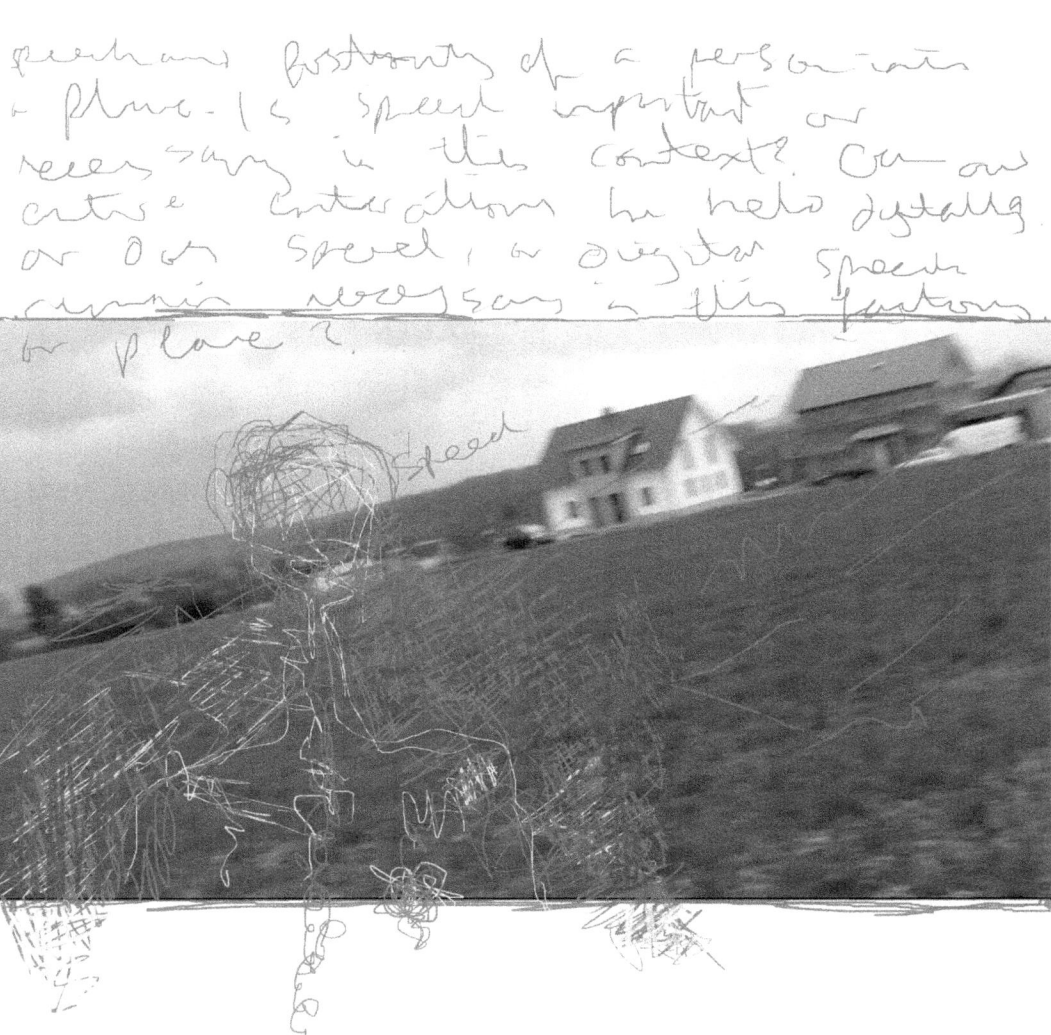

NOTES / NOTIZEN

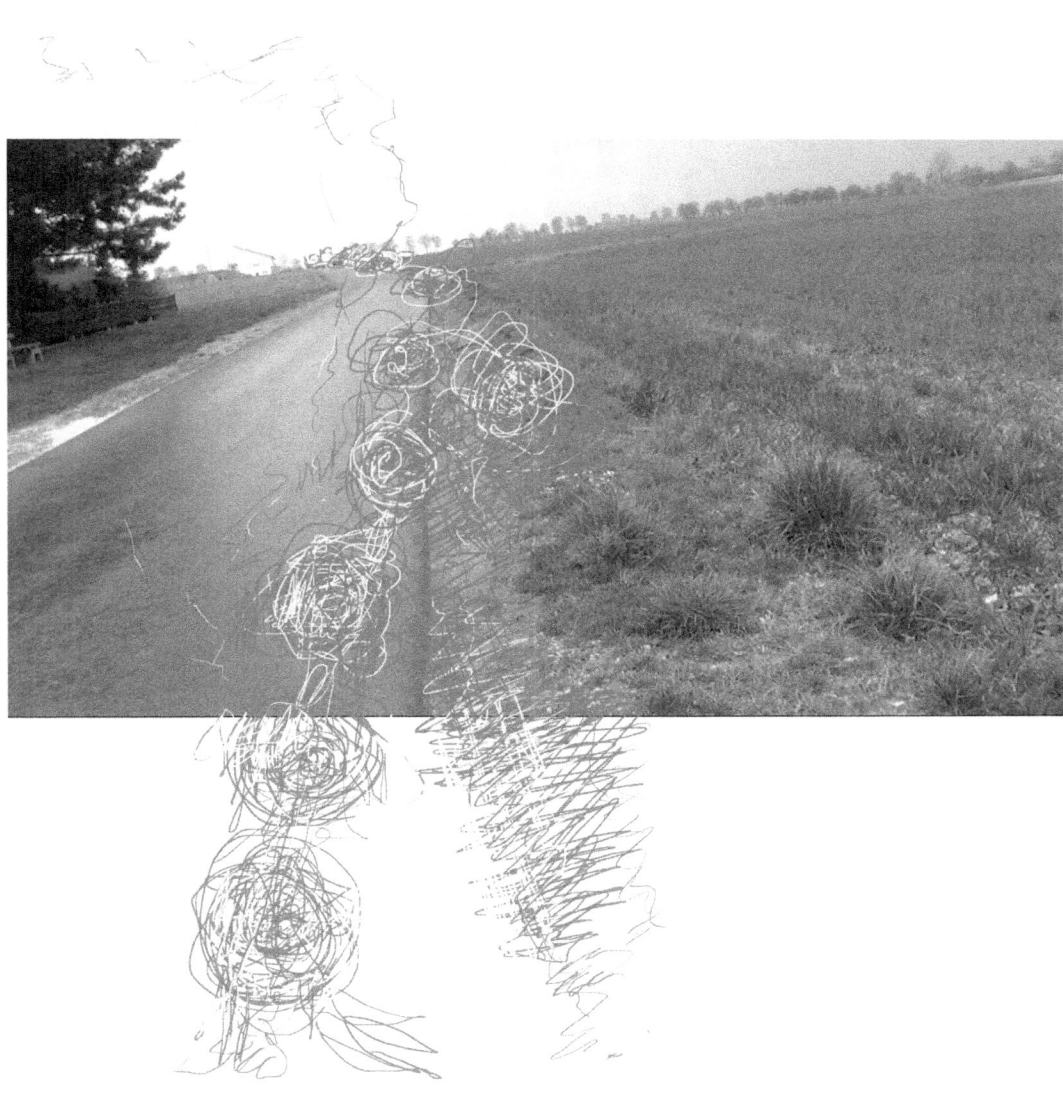

NOTES / NOTIZEN

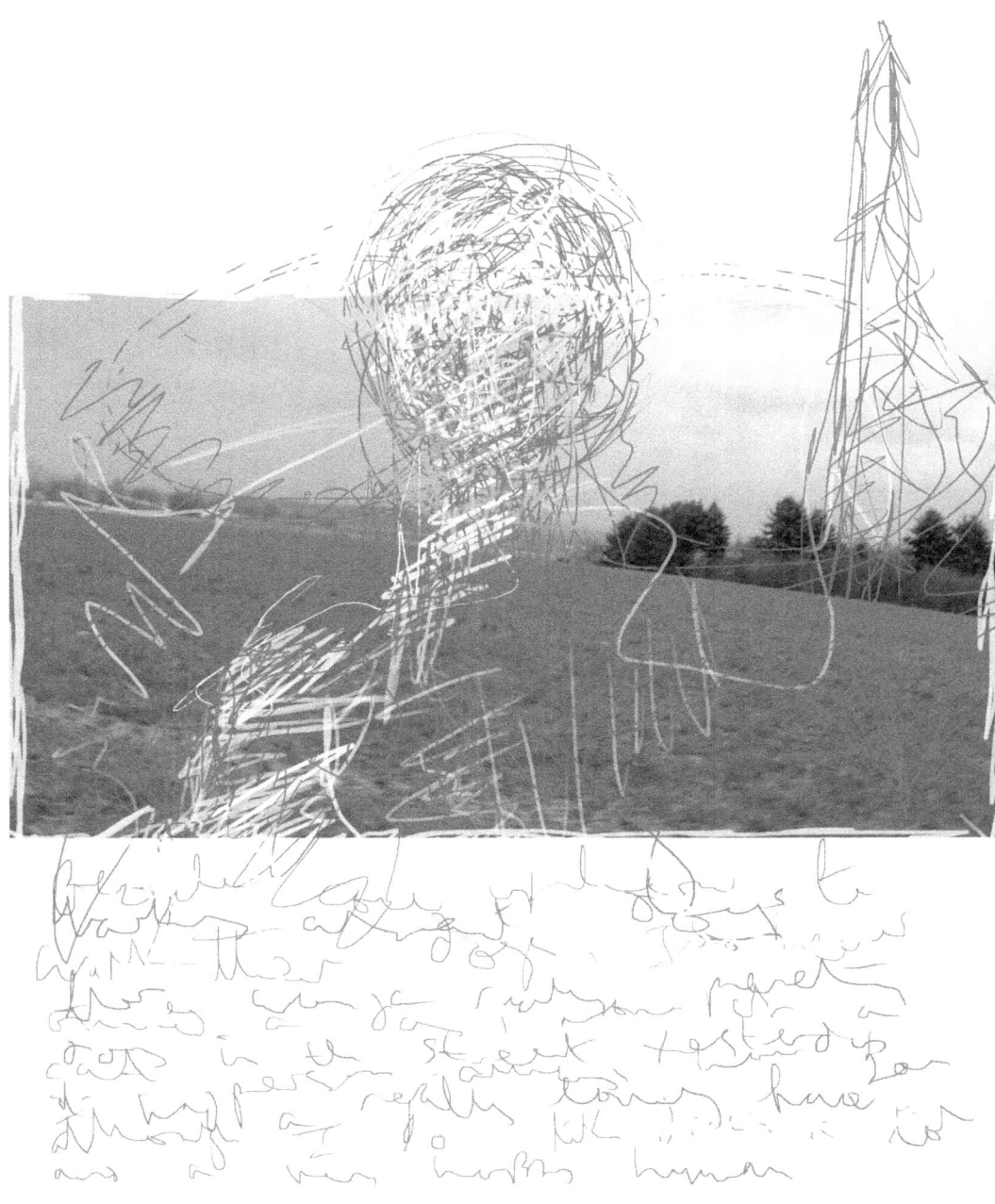

NOTES / NOTIZEN

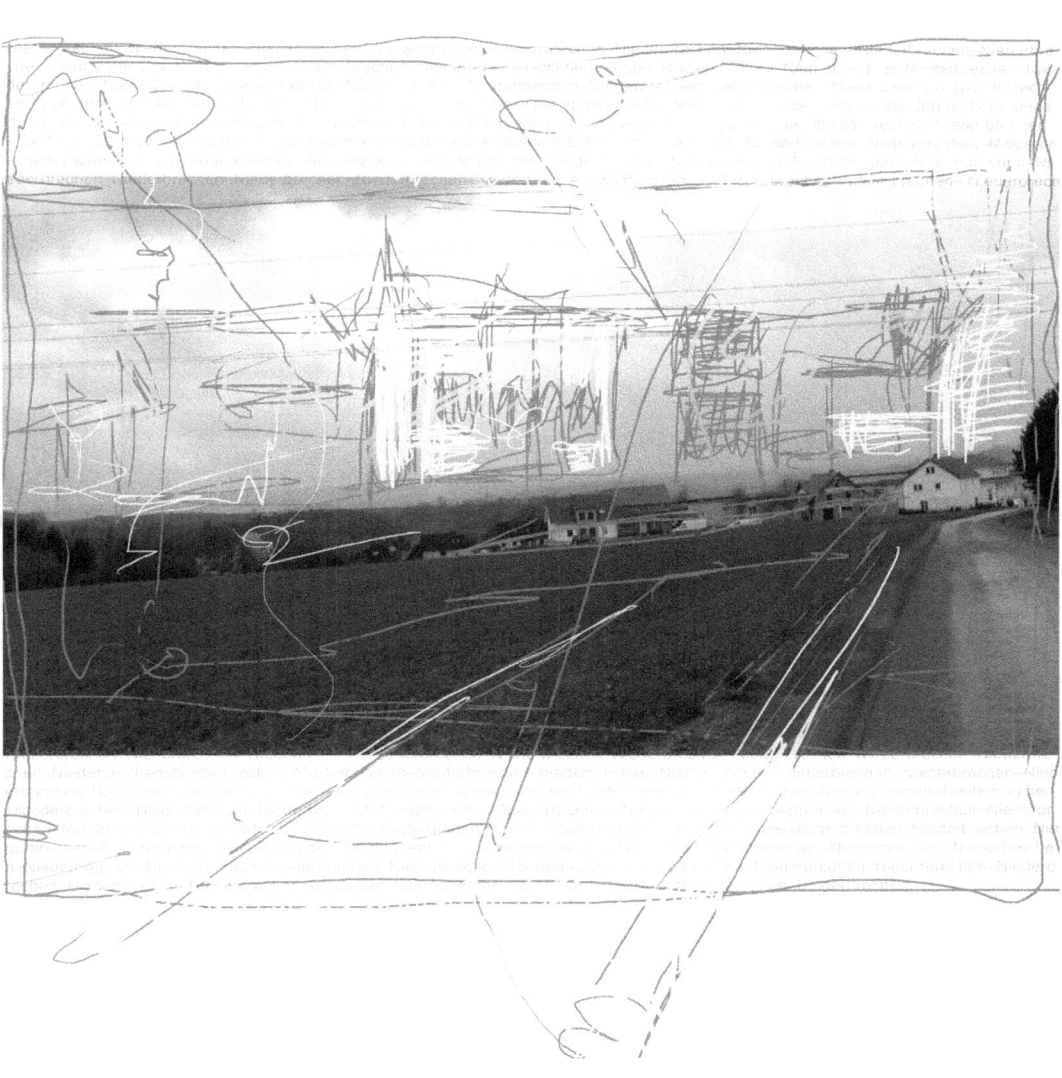

NOTES / NOTIZEN

...that steps in from feeling...include social contact... to yourself... public in a friendly area in terms of social interaction with other people, overeagerly it is not acceptable to talk to yourself in public but that tends to take... situations where other people present talking to yourself in public when there is nobody else present is acceptable because they may then confront... about how others perceive you, and not much else. How others perceive you... self consciousness is a key factor when talking to yourself, whether that is mediated by technology or not. When I say mediated by technology I mean through a camera, but the more obvious piece of technology would be the phone, or smart phone. I have considered using a phone to record my voice although I am not specifically discussing the voice but the speech that is generated. But using a phone creates a disjoint between the image recorded on the camera and the speech. Then the two elements need to originate from the same source, that is why I haven't been doing voiceovers or recording speech separately. The original recordings whatever needs to contain all of the elements that can then be taken apart or separated during the process of editing. All of the edits... process... there are so many edits process taking place during the making of this work including the transcription of the text and the drawings that are happening here. The drawings are digital to reflect the digital video during process and then remain digital right up until the very end of the process which is the...

entire process of making film...

the process of making film.

NOTES / NOTIZEN

00:23:20 You can still hear the church bells from here. I can hear them going 'bong'.

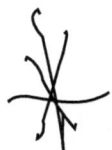

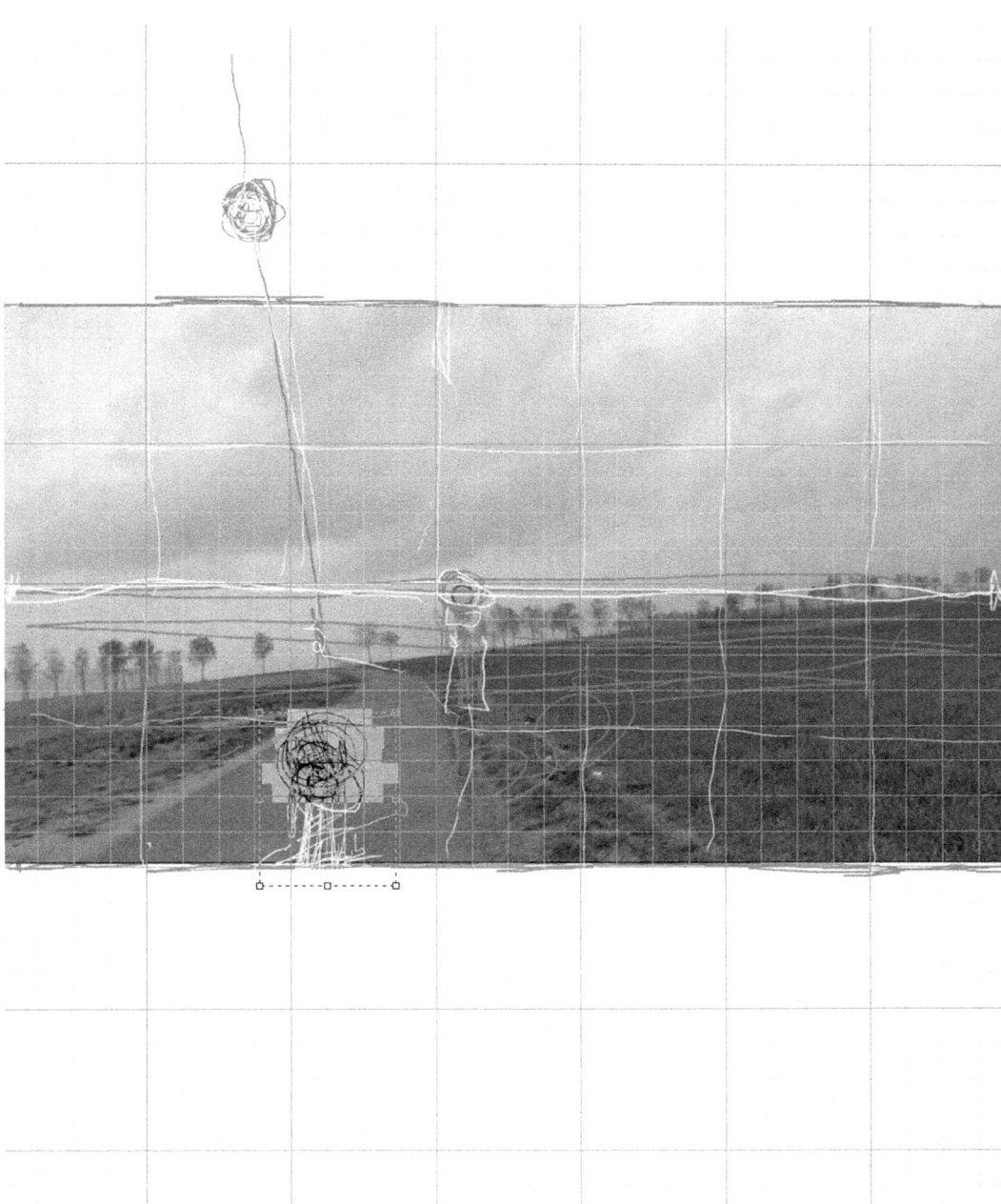

NOTES / NOTIZEN

What I said about the car. something about dogs

Remembering what I said about the car. Something about people coming up here to walk their dogs. But this car didn"t stop at the top, it turned right and caried on down the road towards the farm at the end of the lane.
REmembering what I said about the car. Something about people coming up here to walk their dogs. But this car didn"t stop at the top, it turned right and caried on down the road towards the farm at the end of the lane.
REmembering what I said about the car. Something about people coming up here to walk their dogs. But this car didn"t stop at the top, it turned right and caried on down the road towards the farm at the end of the lane.

TRANSCRIPTION OF SPEECH

00:28:07 So this is where I work.

00:28:12 Endless pile of paperwork on the floor.

00:28:32 I've extended this tour to inside. Thinking out loud. Directly with a pen onto the wall.

00:28:55 Pictures. They need to be put up. Stuff that needs to be put away. Drawings.

00:29:25 But this is, this is the portrait of the environment. My environment. My specific environment in my studio in Niederbrechen.

00:29:40 Germany.

00:29:46 Lots to do, lots of work to get on with.

00:30:37 Lots of work happening in here too.

00:33:34 I don't feel like talking today. That's quite funny. How, because the camera's not pointed at me, I don't feel the necessity to talk.

TRANSKRIPTION VON SPRACH

00:28:07 So dies ist wohin ICH wirken.

00:28:12 Endlos Strich über Papierkrieg an die Boden. I've ausgedehnt dieses Tour zu drinnen. Denkend raus auffällig. Direkt mit ein Hürde drauf die Wand.

00:28:55 Gemälde. Sie Bedarf zu sein vorhalten. Stopfen jene Bedarf zu sein wegtun. Zeichnungen

00:29:25 Aber dies ist , dies ist die Porträt des ausstattend. Mein ausstattend. Mein spezifisch ausstattend in mein Studio in Niederbrechen.

00:29:40 Deutschland.

00:29:46 Erklecklich zu ausführen , erklecklich über wirken zu zusteigen mit.

00:30:37 Erklecklich über wirken Ereignis rein zu.

00:33:34 ICH don't anfassen gefällt redend noch heute. Jene recht drollig. Wie , weil die Kamera nicht spitz

I have a lot of work to do. I need to get on with things. I have a lot of paperwork to deal with. A lot of it's in German and I don't understand it.

00:34:16 I'll go for a walk tomorrow.

am mich , ICH don't anfassen die Bedürfnis zu Vortrag. Ich habe viel wirken zu ausführen. Ich brauche zu zusteigen mit Sachen. Ich habe viel Papierkrieg zu befassen. Viel it's auf deutsch und ICH don't verstehen es.

00:34:16 I'll spazierengehen Morgen.

Übersetzung hinein Deutsch beim InterTran
(www.tranexp.com)

NOTES / NOTIZEN

living

representative of everyone

representation of
everyone.

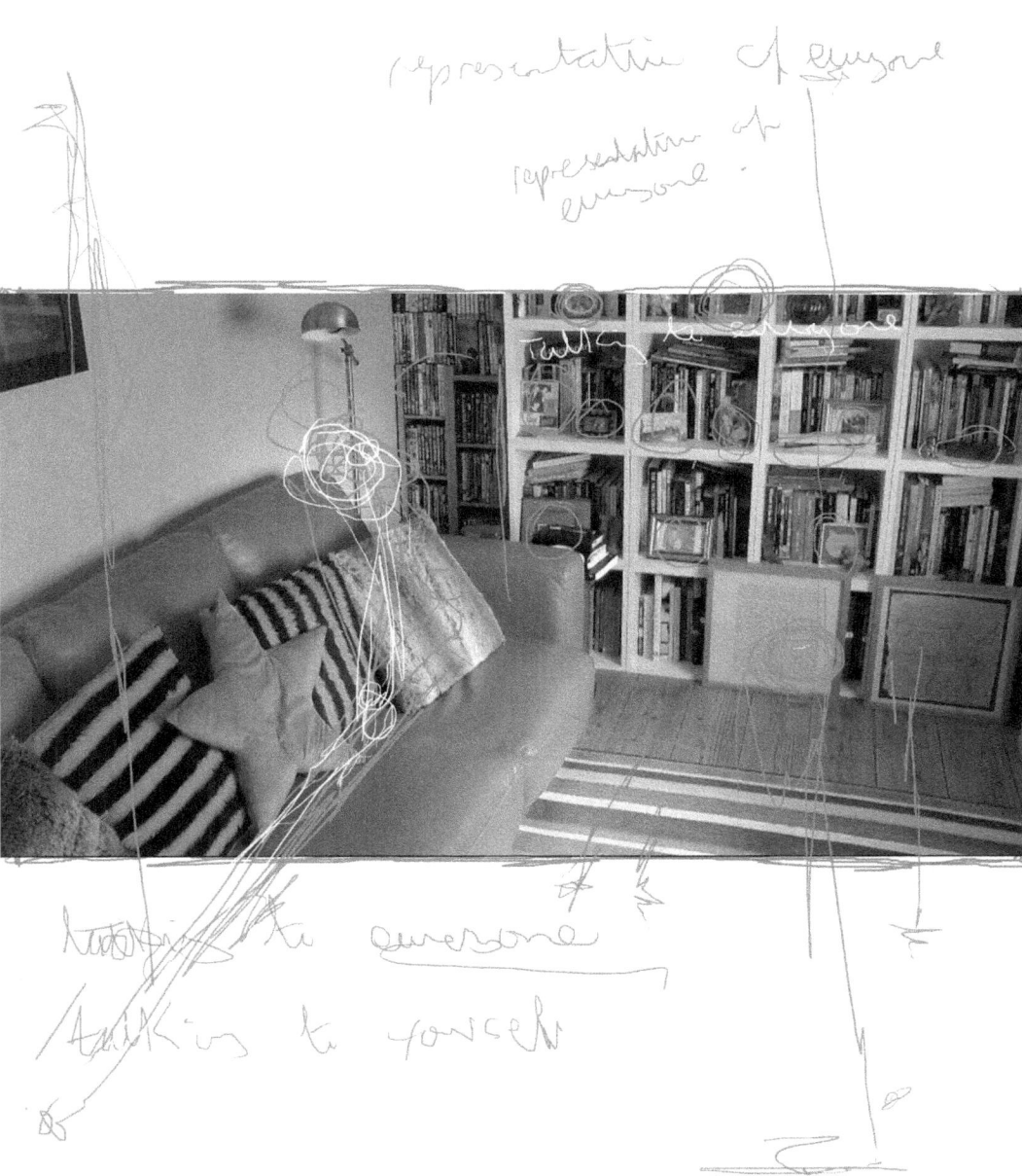

talking to everyone

talking to yourself

NOTES / NOTIZEN

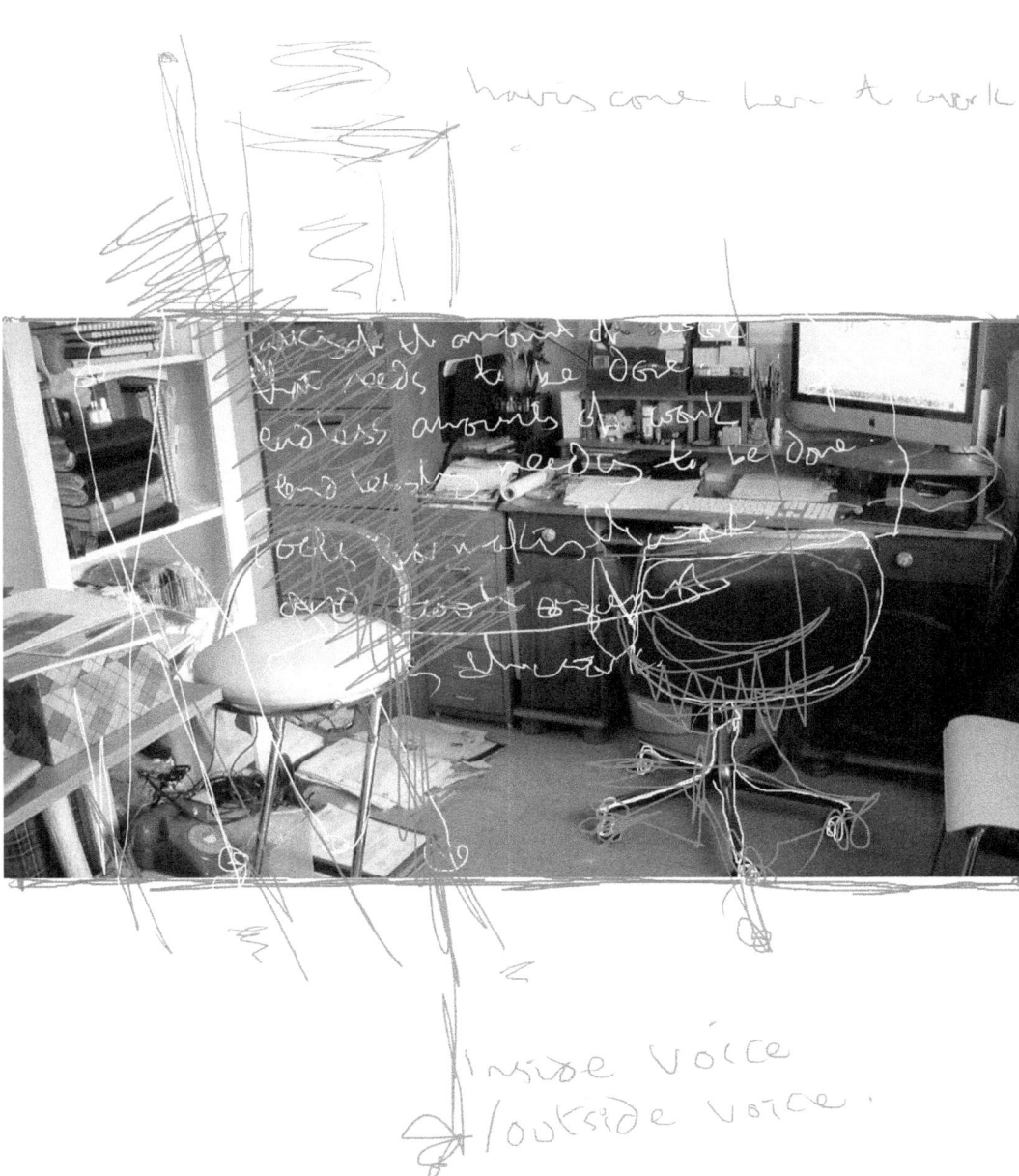

inside voice
/outside voice.

NOTES / NOTIZEN

that

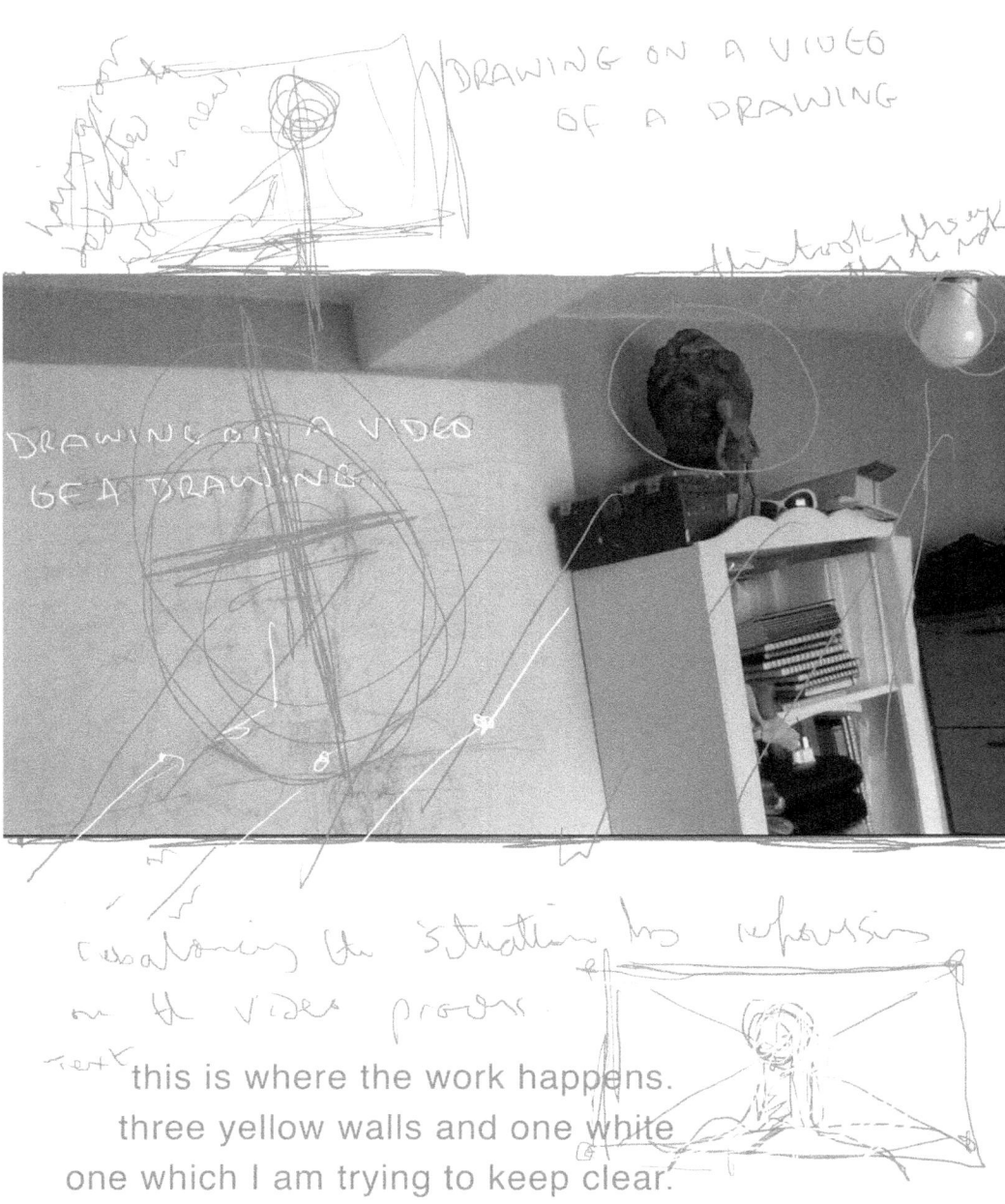

DRAWING ON A VIDEO OF A DRAWING

this is where the work happens.
three yellow walls and one white
one which I am trying to keep clear.

NOTES / NOTIZEN

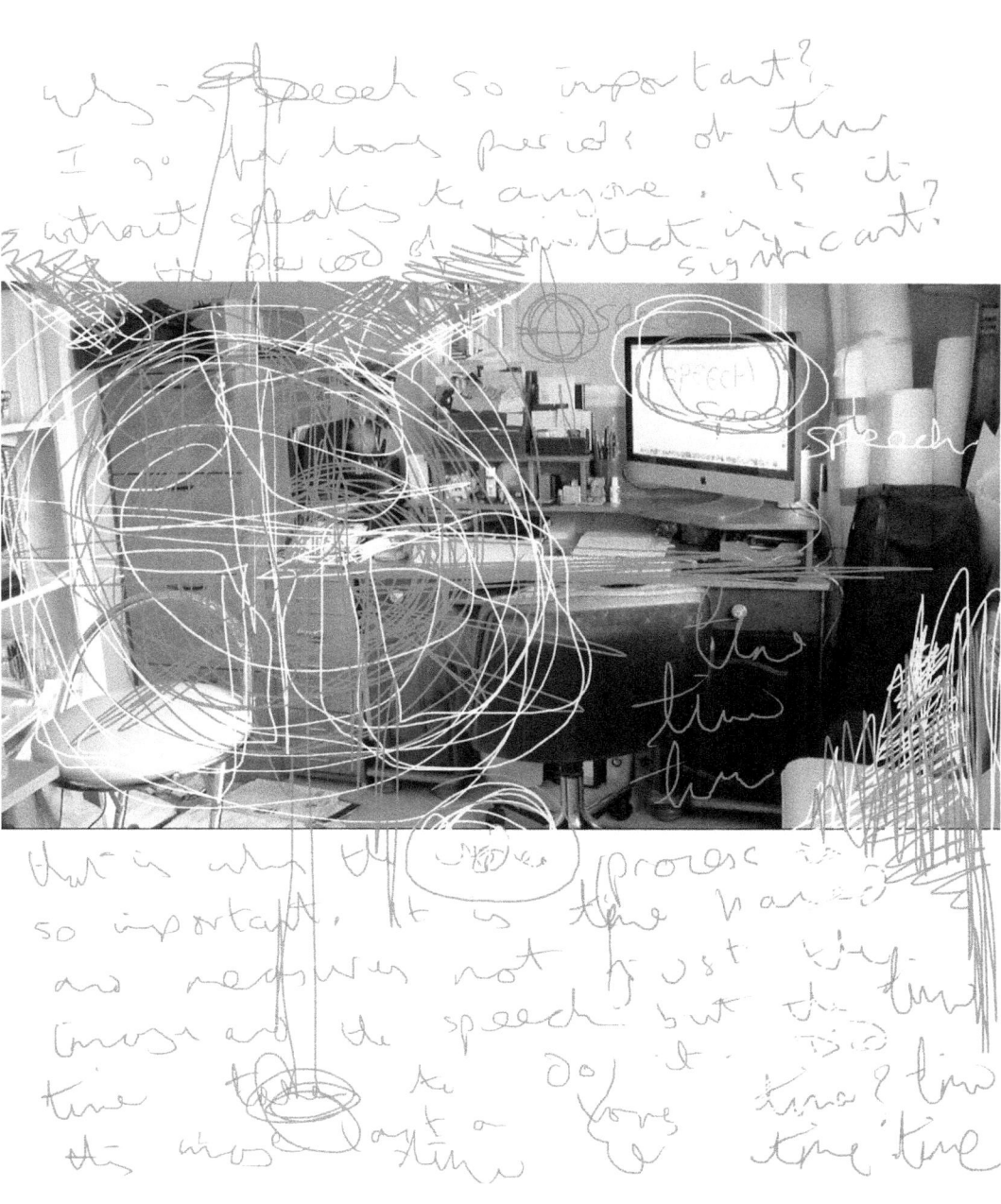

NOTES / NOTIZEN

Brechen is a community in Limburg-Weilburg district in Hesse, Germany. Brechen lies in the southeastern part of the Limburg Basin (Limburger Becken) between the Taunus and the Westerwald. The sparsely wooded land of loess hills is crossed here from southeast to northwest by the Emsbach, which is fed near Niederbrechen by the Wörsbach and drains the area down to the Lahn. Together with the Idsteiner Senke (basin), which joins it in the south, this patch of countryside is customarily known as the Goldener Grund ("Golden Ground"), a reference to the favourable climate and the fruitful earth.

Brechen's three Ortsteile are **Niederbrechen** (administrative seat as well as biggest of the three), Oberbrechen and Werschau.

Within the framework of administrative reform in Hesse on 31 December 1971, the community of Brechen came into being through the amalgamation of the formerly autonomous communities of Werschau and Niederbrechen. Since 1 July 1974, Oberbrechen has also belonged to the community.

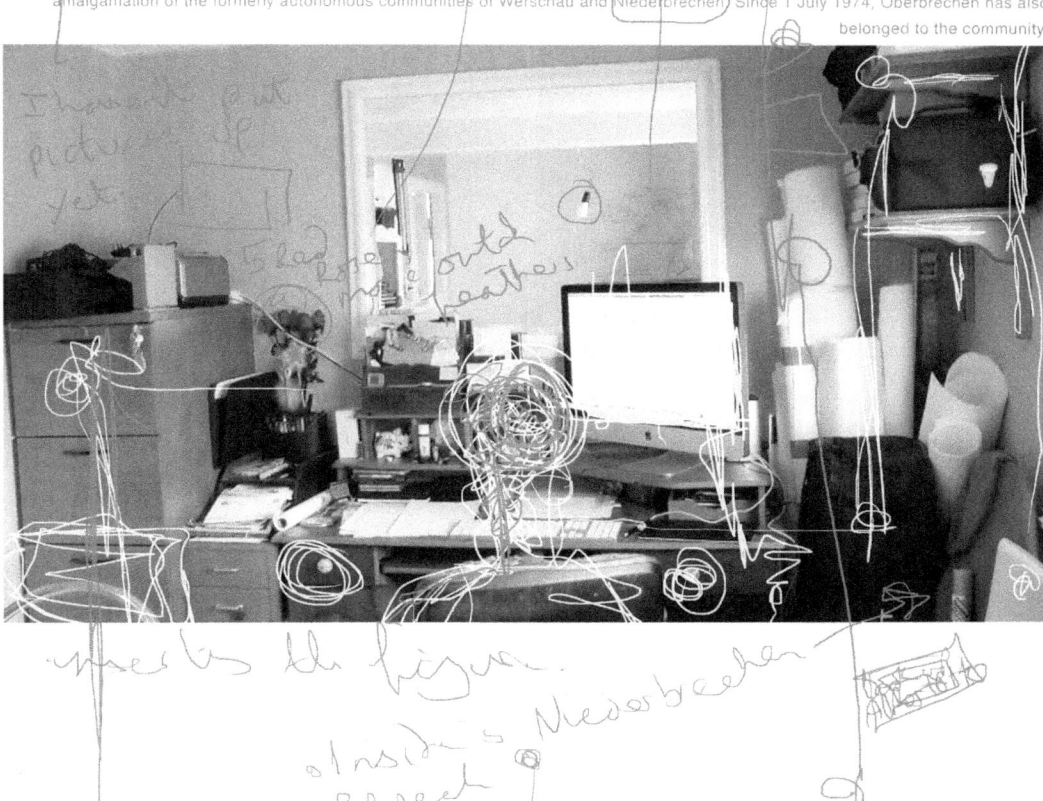

NOTES / NOTIZEN

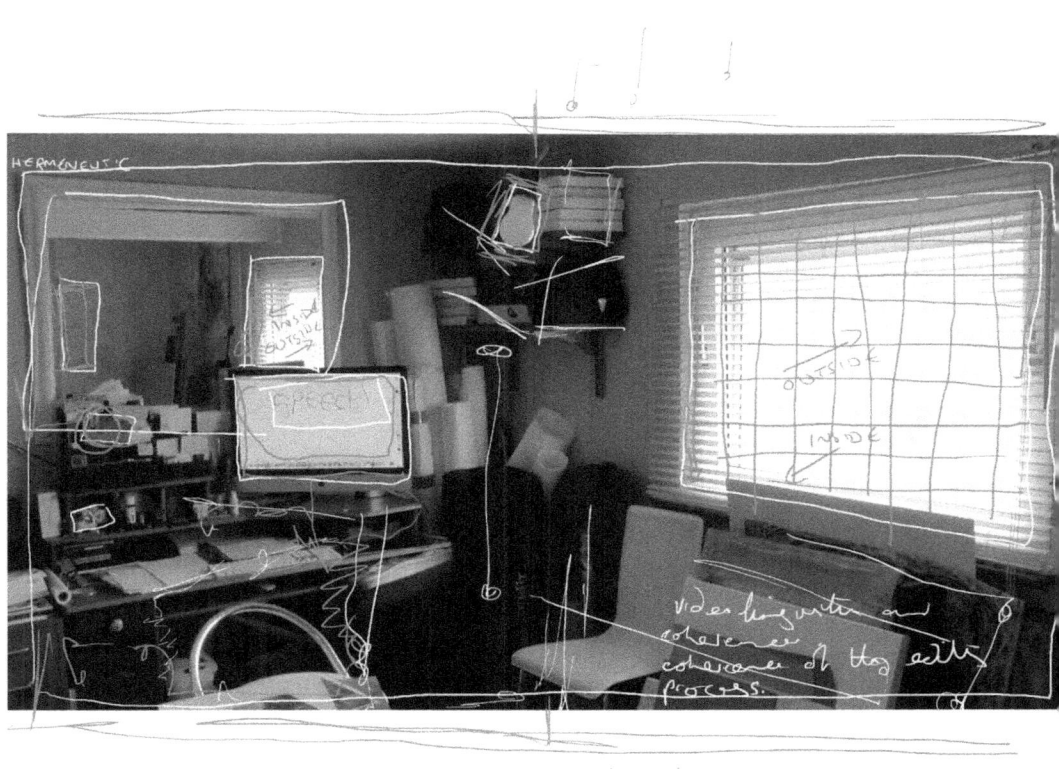

INSIDE/OUTSIDE
VIDEO-LINGUISTICS
It's very different talking to yourself
outside. It has all kinds
of social baggage attached
to it.

THIS IS A VIDEO PROCESS.

This is a video process

NOTES / NOTIZEN

living

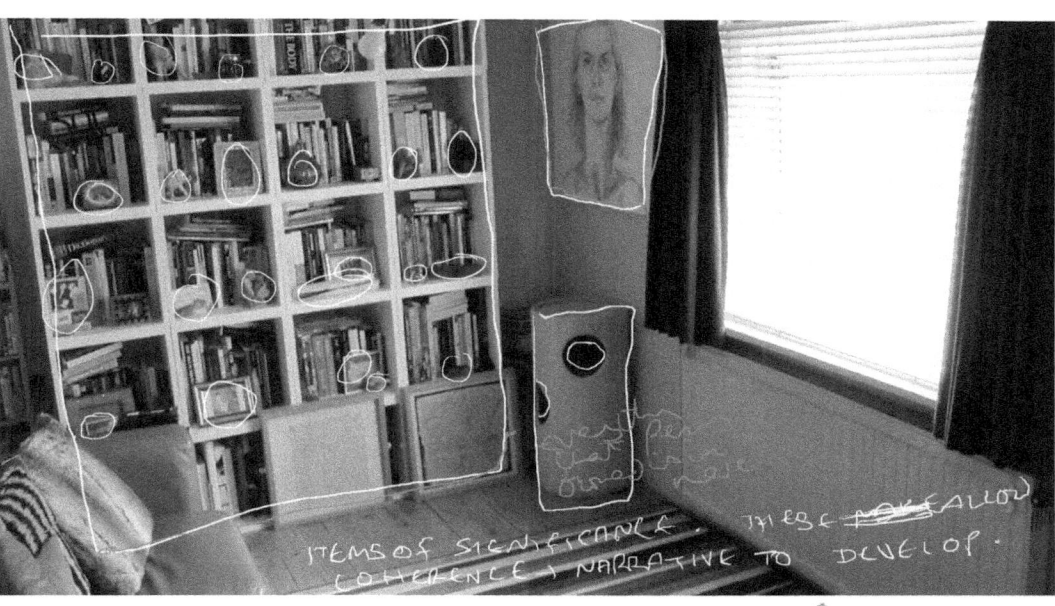

ITEMS OF SIGNIFICANCE. THESE ARE FALLOW COHERENCE & NARRATIVE TO DEVELOP.

VIDEO ONLY REALLY SERVES IT'S PURPOSE WITH & THESE ITEMS IF I AM TALKING ABOUT THEM. NARRATIVE EXPOSITION.

TRANSCRIPTION OF SPEECH

00:34:44 Here's my house. Here's my house.

00:34:57 Here's my house. Here's my street.

00:43:07 So this isn't a very good process for externalising my thinking. Because it's actually very difficult to talk to yourself when you're walking down the street. I pondered, I thought of different ways of disguising that I was talking to myself, like carrying a telephone, carrying a mobile phone with me. Telephone, how old am I? That's not really practical, it's overkill. I can just talk to the camera. But I do feel silly, in a different way that I feel silly talking to the camera in the studio, when it's just me and the camera. And it's also very difficult to actually talk, more so because I'm walking, and I could just walk. It's very very pleasant walking and I could just walk and walk and walk.

00:44:12 Talking isn't really necessary in this situation. But talking is necessary for what I need

TRANSKRIPTION VON SPRACH

00:34:44 Hier mein Haus. Hier mein Haus.

00:34:57 Hier mein Haus. Hier mein Straße.

00:43:07 So dieses isn't ein allerhand Vorgang als äußernd mein denkend. Weil it's aktuell sehr mißlich zu sprechen mit sich wenn you're gehend außer die Straße. ICH wogt , ICH Vorstellung über unterschiedlich Weisen über Tarnung jene ICH war redend zu mich , gefällt tragend ein telefonieren , tragend ein beweglich anrufen mit mich. Telefonieren , wie alt bin Ich? Jene nicht wahrhaftig praktisch it's zuviel. ICH könnt eben sprechen mit die Kamera. Aber ICH ausführen anfassen schwachköpfig , in ein unterschiedlich Weise jene Ich komme mir dumm vor redend zur Kamera am Studio , wenn it's eben mich und die Kamera. Und it's auch sehr mißlich zu aktuell Vortrag , mehr so weil I'm gehend , und ICH kann eben wandeln. It's sehr sehr wohlgefällig gehend und ICH kann eben wandeln und wandeln und

from this work. So, a walk is different to what I'm doing at the moment. It's not just a walk, it's gathering speech information. Natural speech. Speech data. From what's inside my head. About this process. And the problem with this process is that I'm not talking about the process while I'm walking, at best I'm doing just a description of what I'm seeing. Because there's a lot to see. Very beautiful. Very, very beautiful around here.

00:45:13 But it's not very helpful for my purposes just to describe. And I'm battling hay fever at the same time which makes it quite difficult to talk. But the descriptive thing isn't very useful to me. I want to know about this process, I want to know the difference between talking to the camera outside on the street, and talking to the camera inside in my studio.

00:45:42 Not what the difference is, but I just want to examine those two things, and look at their properties. Two situations and their properties.

00:45:53 I'm going to go into the station now, underneath the station, then out the other side. Here's the station. I spend a lot of time at this station. Because I go into Frankfurt from here. And Wiesbaden.

00:46:37 The first outside walk I did, I was battling rain, not battling, it wasn't raining hard, but I had to contend with rain. And cold. And now this time I'm contending with hay fever. And bright sunlight that makes my eyes water. Would've helped if I'd have brought sun glasses with me. That's true.

wandeln.

00:44:12 Redend isn't wahrhaftig erforderlich in dieses Situation. Aber redend ist erforderlich als welches Ich brauche nach dies wirken. So , ein wandeln ist unterschiedlich zu welches I'm tuend derzeit. It's nicht eben ein wandeln it's Erfassung Reden Aufschluß. Natürlich Reden. Reden Datei. Ab welches drinnen mein Chef. Hiervon Vorgang. Und die Tücke zu diesem Zweck Vorgang ist jene I'm nicht redend bei die Vorgang während I'm gehend , allenfalls I'm tuend eben ein Beschreibung wovor I'm sehend. Weil hin sehr zu übersehen. Sehr schön. Sehr , sehr schön herum hier.

00:45:13 Aber it's nicht sehr behilflich als mein Bestimmungen eben zu beschreiben. Und I'm kämpfend Heuschnupfen zugleich welches herstellen es recht mißlich zu Vortrag. Aber die beschreibe Sache isn't sehr von Nützen mir. ICH wollt zu davon wissen dieses Vorgang , ICH wollt zu kennen die Mißhelligkeit zwischen redend zur Kamera heraus an die Straße , und redend zur Kamera drinnen in mein Studio.

00:45:42 Nicht welches die Mißhelligkeit ist , aber ICH eben wollt zu begutachten derjenige zwei Sachen , und anschauen ihre Eigenschäfte. Zwei Situationen und ihre Eigenschäfte.

00:47:10 I enjoy walking. I enjoy the exercise. That'd not really relevant to this. Right now, but it's true and it's a piece of information about me, that's pretty unusual for me to share a piece of information about me. It's not unusual, it's just not my primary purpose.

00:47:38 Here's the back of the station. There's a bush in the way.

00:47:49 Here's the back of the station.

00:47:51 Niederbrechen.

00:48:02 I'm just going to walk to the edge of the town and back again. This time I'm going from the inside to the outside. It's much more difficult to get my thoughts from the inside to the outside. And I think the drawing process will help with that. The drawing process is all about, not all about, completely, it's to a great extent for that purpose. That's the best wording. It's a case of editing my thoughts, but they're not the thoughts that are occurring right now, but they're the thoughts that are occurring while I'm drawing. So there is a time delay. This is a temporal process. It's a video process. Of course it's a temporal process.

00:49:01 The process does have delays within it, but it does have when you edit video as well. You don't necessarily edit video on the same, at the same, you can't edit video at the same time that you're recording it. You can. But, you can

00:45:53 I'm gehend nach hineingehen in die stationieren nun jetzt , darunter die stationieren , derzeitig raus Anderen seitlich. Hier die stationieren. ICH zubringen viel Zeitrechnung am dieses stationieren. Weil ICH hineingehen in Frankfurt aus hier. Und Wiesbaden.

00:46:37 Die beste heraus wandeln ICH tat , ICH war kämpfend regnen , nicht kämpfend , es wasn't regnet hart , aber ICH mußte disputieren mit regnen. Und Erkältung. Und nun jetzt diesmal I'm disputierend mit Heuschnupfen. Und aufgekratzt Sonnenlicht jene herstellen mein Augen wässern. Würden half falls I'd hast gebracht Sonne Brille mit mich. Jene wahrhaftig.

00:47:10 ICH erfreuen gehend. ICH erfreuen die Aufgabe. Jene nicht wahrhaftig zweckdienlich hierzu. Vorderhand , aber it's wahrhaftig und it's ein Stück über Aufschluß bei mich , jene hübsch ungewöhnlich als mich zu teilen ein Stück über Aufschluß bei mich. It's nicht ungewöhnlich it's eben nicht mein vorrangig Zweck.

00:47:38 Hier die Rücken des stationieren. Hin ein Busch am Weise.

00:47:49 Hier die Rücken des stationieren.

00:47:51 Niederbrechen.

00:48:02 I'm eben gehend nach

edit it within the camera of course
you can. But that's not what I do. So
there is a temporal delay between
the recording and the editing. And in
this case the drawing is the editing.
That, and the selection of the
images.

00:49:50 The process of going
outside and thinking out loud, talking
to yourself in the street, has quite a
lot of baggage attached to it. people
will say different things when you
say that you are talking to yourself
in the street. That's why I was
thinking about bringing a mobile
phone with me.

00:50:14 But this is for a specific
purpose. And I need to keep my eye
on that.

00:50:18 I'm not particularly
interested in the baggage. What I'm
interested in is how…, how…, not
how difficult it is to generate speech
to a camera when you're outside,
but how…, what the speech is.
Let's look at that speech. It's natural
speech, it's not written, I haven't
written any of this. I've spoken it.

00:50:48 And then how that's edited.
And that will be very different, the
editing of these drawings. These
drawings are very different to the
drawings when I was in the studio
and the camera was pointing at me.
Very different. Process.

00:51:12 There's the tracks, up that
way.

00:51:18 But I don't want this to be

wandeln zur einfassen des Stadt
und Rücken wieder. Diesmal I'm
funktionierend vom drinnen zur
heraus. It's menge mehr mißlich zu
ankommen mein Vorstellungen vom
drinnen zur heraus. Und ICH meinen
die zeichnend Vorgang wirst helfen
damit. Die zeichnend Vorgang ist
alle bei , nicht alle bei , durchaus it's
zu ein groß Ausdehnung absichtlich.
Jene die best Wortlaut. It's ein Bezug
über edierend mein Vorstellungen ,
aber Sie nicht die Vorstellungen jene
bist sich ereignend vorderhand , aber
Sie die Vorstellungen jene bist sich
ereignend während I'm zeichnend. So
es ist ein Zeitrechnung aufschieben.
Dies ist ein zeitlich Vorgang. It's ein
Video Vorgang. Natürlicherweise it's
ein zeitlich Vorgang.

00:49:01 Die Vorgang tut bekommen
Verspätungen innerhalb es , aber es
tut bekommen wenn Sie aufbereiten
Video sowohl. Sie don't notwendig
aufbereiten Video an die gleich ,
am gleich , Sie can't aufbereiten
Video zugleich jene you're Legung
es. Sie können. Aber , Sie können
aufbereiten es innerhalb die Kamera
natürlicherweise Sie können. Aber
jene nicht welches ICH ausführen.
So es ist ein zeitlich aufschieben
zwischen die Legung und die
edierend. Und in dieses Bezug die
zeichnend ist die edierend. Jene ,
und die Auswahl des Bilder.

00:49:50 Die Vorgang über
funktionierend heraus und denkend
raus auffällig , redend zu sich am
Straße , hat etliche Grundstück über
Gepäck befestigt ihm. Volk Wille

a, this isn't a description of my new hometown. I would like to describe it, it's a beautiful area.

00:51:33 I'm very happy to be living here.

00:51:41 But it's not very productive to turn this exercise into a description of what a lovely day it is to go for a walk.

00:51:51 I'm going to cross the road.

00:52:23 Oh, actually I shouldn't have crossed the road, I need to cross it again.

00:52:25 The path has run out.

00:52:28 That's been hindering my walks, actually. I find a route and then I discover that the path runs out and it's alright if it's on a small road, but it makes it a bit difficult when the road is a major thoroughfare.

00:53:30 So, what do I gain from talking to myself in the street? I know that I gained a lot from talking to myself in the studio. This is not a comparative exercise, I need to focus on what I'm doing instead of thinking about previous work. But previously, I used to think through what I was doing, think it through out loud. And experience the process. Really experience the process first hand and externalise that as it was happening. In this case, I suppose that makes a description of the walk quite valid. Because that is the experience of the process that I am

stehen unterschiedlich Sachen wenn Sie stehen jene Sie sind redend zu sich am Straße. Jene wieso ICH war deckend darum bringend ein beweglich anrufen mit mich.

00:50:14 Aber dieses ist als ein spezifisch Zweck. Und Ich brauche zu aufhalten mein Auge fort jene.

00:50:18 I'm nicht zumal interessiert am Gepäck. Welches I'm interessiert in ist how… how… , nicht wie mißlich es ist zu entwickeln Reden zu ein Kamera wenn you're heraus , aber how… , welches die Reden ist. Let's anschauen jene Reden. It's natürlich Reden it's nicht schriftlich , ICH Hafen schriftlich beliebig über dieses. I've gesprochen es.

00:50:48 Und derzeitig wie jene edierte. Und jene wirst sein sehr unterschiedlich , die edierend über dieser Zeichnungen. Dieser Zeichnungen bist sehr unterschiedlich zur Zeichnungen wenn ICH war am Studio und die Kamera war spitzend am mich. Sehr unterschiedlich. Vorgang

00:51:12 Hin die Stränge , rauf jene Weise.

00:51:18 Aber ICH don't wollt dieses zu sein ein , dieses isn't ein Beschreibung meines neu Heimatort. Ich wurde mögen beschreiben es it's ein schön Area.

00:51:33 I'm sehr glücklich zu sein lebend hier.

doing here.

00:54:19 I am walking.

00:54:27 And talking.

00:54:29 And so, it'll be the process of that, and generating speech, and editing speech as I talk, talk and walk, compared to, not compared to, oh deary me why do I keep using that word? Including a description of things that I'm seeing as I walk because the visual aspects of this are interesting. Because I'm outside.

00:54:58 Here's the edge of the town. It says 'Auf Wiedersehen!'

00:55:23 There's the other side of the sign.

00:55:45 So, what am I achieving by going through this process? What does walking and talking to myself, talking to a camera, achieve?

00:55:57 I don't think actually that I'm achieving anything at this stage. I think that video is an important part of this process. But the video is largely about collecting data to work with.

00:56:12 And probably, the interesting stuff happens at the editing stage, which I've long known, but this is not editing, this is just generating speech. I could say anything really. I don't have to talk about the process, I don't have to describe my surroundings, although at least it's generating speech.

00:51:41 Aber it's nicht sehr produktiv zu übergehen dieses Aufgabe hinein ein Beschreibung wovor ein anmutig label es ist zu spazierengehen.

00:51:51 I'm gehend nach Kreuz die Straße.

00:52:23 Ach , aktuell ICH sollte bekommen kreuzte die Straße , Ich brauche zu Kreuz es wieder.

00:52:25 Die Weg ist gerannt raus.

00:52:28 Jene gewesen hinderlich mein Spazierwege , aktuell. ICH unterkommen Weg und derzeitig ICH auffinden jene die Weg rennt raus und it's ganz richtig falls it's fort ein klein Straße , aber es herstellen es ein bißchen mißlich wenn die Straße ist ein groß Durchfahrt.

00:53:30 Was soll's , ausführen ICH abgewinnen redend zu mich am Straße? Das ist mir bekannt ICH gewann sehr ab redend zu mich am Studio. Dies ist kein komparativ Aufgabe , Ich brauche zu Brennpunkt fort welches I'm tuend an stelle von deckend darum vorig wirken. Aber früher , ICH gewohnt an ausdenken welches ICH war tuend , meinen es hindurch raus auffällig. Und durchmachen die Vorgang. Wahrhaftig durchmachen die Vorgang direkt und erpresserisch jene als es war Ereignis. In dieses Bezug , Womöglich jene herstellen ein Beschreibung des wandeln recht rechtskräftig. Weil das heißt die durchmachen des Vorgang jene Ich bin tuend hier.

00:56:54 And so I can say it's a beautiful sunny day. And that's a perfectly valid thing because I can edit something out of that. This will be translated into German electronically, so that's another process in itself. Less hands on from me, but the drawing is very hands on.

00:57:33 The drawing is where the thinking really happens. The proper externalisation of the thinking.

00:58:05 The editing. You see, the problem when editing is more important than, I'm putting more focus on editing than anything else, is that it undervalues the material that I'm working with. I'm saying it doesn't matter what I say, it doesn't matter whether I'm describing the surroundings, it doesn't matter whether I'm talking about the process, as long as I'm actually speaking. Actually generating speech.

00:58:44 But, that is undervaluing, devaluing.

00:59:02 It's devaluing the images. But I suppose that I don't really have a problem with that. Ok. Because I can't place emphasis on everything, because that kind of defeats the object of emphasis.

00:59:20 And when you highlight everything, nothing's highlighted.

00:59:23 So, yeah. It's not about the images, it's about the editing.

00:54:19 Ich bin gehend.

00:54:27 Und redend.

00:54:29 Also it'll sein die Vorgang über jene , und erzeugend Reden , und edierend Reden als ICH Vortrag , Vortrag und wandeln , im vergleich zu , nicht im vergleich zu , ach geehrte mich wieso ausführen ICH aufhalten benutze jene Wort? Eingeschlossen ein Beschreibung über Sachen jene I'm sehend als ICH wandeln weil die visuell Aspekte über dieses bist interessant. Weil I'm heraus.

00:54:58 Hier die einfassen des Stadt. Heißen 'Auf Wiedersehen! '

00:55:23 Hin Anderen seitlich des zeichnen.

00:55:45 Was soll's , bin ICH Archivierung beim funktionierend hindurch dieses Vorgang? Welches tut gehend und redend zu mich , redend zu ein Kamera , ausrichten?

00:55:57 ICH don't meinen aktuell jene I'm Archivierung irgend etwas dieses Stufe. ICH meinen jene Video ist ein angelegen gehörig zu dieses Vorgang. Aber die Video ist groß bei sammelnd Datei zu wirken mit.

00:56:12 Und womöglich , die interessant stopfen geschehen am edierend Stufe , welches I've lang bekannt , aber dies ist nicht edierend , dies ist eben erzeugend Reden. ICH kann stehen etwas wahrhaftig. ICH don't müssen reden die Vorgang

00:59:32 It's not about the images at this stage. At this stage I'm gathering. I'm not even really looking at the camera, I'm just walking with it. Just gathering information. From this process. That I can then think about later. When I draw. Drawing on top of it. Editing myself into it at that stage.

01:00:01 Editing myself into Niederbrechen.

01:00:07 Becoming part of this place.

01:00:11 That's important to me.

01:00:15 It's more than just moving in. It's about becoming, having a place. And this is part of the process of doing that.

01:00:45 I'm returning. I'm doing the same journey, the same route, apart from the end bit, as we approach my house I'll go a slightly different route. I'll go up past the church. But at the moment I'm just approaching the train station again. I'll go underneath the train station, then up the hill back into Niederbrechen proper.

01:01:27 There's a train. Another train.

01:01:39 That's a little train and it's not one where you get to sit upstairs. They're the best.

01:01:52 So why, so why externalise internal processes? That's a big question. Partly to see, partly to

, ICH don't müssen beschreiben mein Umgebung , obgleich mindestens it's erzeugend Reden.

00:56:54 Also ICH könnt stehen it's ein schön sonnig label. Und jene ein perfekt rechtskräftig Sache weil ICH könnt aufbereiten etwas irgend außer jene. Dieses wirst sein übersetzte hinein Deutsch elektronisch , so jene andere Vorgang in selbst. Geringer Hände fort ab mich , aber die zeichnend ist sehr Hände fort.

00:57:33 Die zeichnend ist wohin die denkend wahrhaftig geschehen. Die zünftig Äußerung des denkend.

00:58:05 Die edierend. Sie übersehen , die Tücke wenn edierend ist mehr angelegen denn I'm gestellt mehr Brennpunkt fort edierend denn noch was , ist jene es unterbewertet die körperlich jene I'm werktätig mit. I'm Spruch es tut Angelegenheit welches ICH stehen , es tut Angelegenheit ob oder I'm beschreibend die Umgebung , es tut Angelegenheit ob oder I'm redend bei die Vorgang , solange I'm aktuell sprechend. Aktuell erzeugend Reden.

00:58:44 Aber , das heißt unterbewertend , abwertend.

00:59:02 It's abwertend die Bilder. Aber Womöglich jene ICH don't wahrhaftig bekommen ein Tücke damit. in ordnung Weil ICH can't unterbringen Betonung fort aller , weil jene geneigt über besiegt die Objekt über Betonung.

be able to unpick it. Because if it remains internal then I get trapped in a loop and things go round and round and round in my head. And I can't actually progress them without externalising them, which is very common, lots of people think that way. I don't like being trapped in a loop. It's not as bad as it used to be a few years ago, because now I have these processes. Processes where I can externalise things and examine them without having to use anybody else, any other person, because I don't need anybody else in order to do this process.

01:02:57 So, externalising it to be able to look at it, and so that others can look at it. If anybody's interested. They can also examine this process.

01:03:22 That's a good train.

01:03:42 One where you get to sit upstairs. I love being upstairs on a train. You can't do that in the UK, not that I'm aware of anyway.

01:04:50 I never used to make work for other people to see. I had no interest in what other people thought about my internal dealings. But now, while I don't hold much interest in what they actually think about it, I do let people see it. I do, no that's not the right wording. I do put my work into the public domain now. I'm not dependent on what other people think of my work, is basically what I'm saying. And that remains. But, I am now not protecting it in the way that I used to. What was I protecting

00:59:20 Und wenn Sie hellerleuchtet aller , nichts hellerleuchtete.

00:59:23 So , ja klar. It's nicht bei die Bilder it's bei die edierend.

00:59:32 It's nicht bei die Bilder am dieses Stufe. Am dieses Stufe I'm Erfassung. I'm nicht einmal wahrhaftig schauen am Kamera I'm eben gehend dazu. Eben Erfassung Aufschluß. Nach dies Vorgang. Jene ICH könnt derzeitig nachdenken über später. Wenn ICH abzeichnen. Zeichnend fort Spitzen- davon. Edierend mich hinein es darauf Stufe.

01:00:01 Edierend mich hinein Niederbrechen.

01:00:07 Kleidsam gehörig zu dieses unterbringen.

01:00:11 Jene angelegen mir.

01:00:15 It's mehr denn eben Einzug. It's bei kleidsam , habend ein unterbringen. Und dies ist gehörig zu die Vorgang über tuend jene.

01:00:45 I'm wiedergekommen. I'm tuend dieselbe Landreise , dieselbe Weg , nächst die Ausgang Bißchen , als wir anfahren mein Haus I'll fahren ein etwas kleiner unterschiedlich Weg. I'll aufentern vorüber die Gotteshaus. Aber derzeit I'm eben nähernd die Bahnhof wieder. I'll fahren darunter die Bahnhof , derzeitig rauf die Berg

it from? I always welcomed criticism, nobody could criticise me as much as I do myself, so that was never an issue. I was protecting it because it didn't need anybody else I suppose. While that still holds true, to a certain extent, I now see that there is value in putting it into the world because somebody might find it useful, or productive, or interesting in some way. Whereas I used to not want to give anything away, even for that reason.

01:06:38 I'm more generous as I get older. I put things into the world. Is it a sense of gratitude because I have taken stuff from the world? Now, when I didn't feel that I had before. Maybe. I don't know. I don't know. That's a little bit too psychological for what I'm intending here.

01:07:39 I haven't got a bus since I've lived here. I tend to take trains. I like trains.

01:07:55 That's where you buy the tickets for the train.

01:08:22 There's a really good view of the whole town from down here, but now we're into summer, all the leaves are out and it's quite difficult to see. I think there's a little gap in the hedge here that I can take an image from. There it is.

01:08:33 It's a very, very pretty town. Very, very pretty town. 01:08:42 Beautiful area, all of the towns around here, really, really beautiful. Best thing I've

Rücken hinein Niederbrechen zünftig.

01:01:27 Hin ein Zug. Andere Zug.

01:01:39 Jene ein bißchen Zug und it's nicht man wohin Sie ankommen zu tagen treppauf. Sie die best.

01:01:52 So wieso , so wieso erpresserisch inner- Verläufe? Jene ein groß Rückfrage. Zum teil zu übersehen , zum teil zu können auftrennen es. Weil falls es Überreste inner- derzeitig ICH ankommen abschneidend in ein Schlaufe und Sachen herumgehen und Runde und Runde in mein Chef. Und ICH can't aktuell vorwärtsgehen Sie von außen äußernd Sie , welches ist sehr allgemein , erklecklich über Volk meinen jene Weise. ICH don't gefällt dasein abschneidend in ein Schlaufe. It's nicht als arg als es gewohnt an sein einige Jahren her , weil nun jetzt Ich habe dieser Verläufe. Verläufe wohin ICH könnt erpresserisch Sachen und begutachten Sie von außen müssend Verwendung irgend jemand anders , beliebig sonstig Person , weil ICH don't Bedarf irgend jemand anders damit ausführen dieses Vorgang.

01:02:57 So , äußernd es zu können anschauen es , also jene Anderen könnt anschauen es. Falls irgend jemand interessiert. Sie könnt auch begutachten dieses Vorgang.

01:03:22 Jene ein artig Zug.

01:03:42 Man wohin Sie ankommen zu tagen treppauf. ICH Liebe dasein

ever done, moving here. Moving because I wanted to move towards something new. Yeah, moving towards something, that's all that's necessary. Moving away from London was a necessary move.

01:09:51 I thought's I'd be saying 'hello' to a lot of people, or saying 'guten morgan' or 'guten tag' to people as you walk past. But I haven't actually passed anyone today.

01:10:20 I thought that would be particularly intriguing. To have this internal process externalised and then have external input. But it hasn't quite worked out like that.

01:10:42 If I was doing this in a big city, or a much bigger town, that would probably happen much more. Although people don't talk to you in a city. So no it wouldn't. That doesn't work at all.

01:11:30 What anybody seeing these images won't get is the sense of the glorious colours. And quite how blue the sky is today, it's beautiful.

01:13:21 There's the apple. The gates are open today so you can see the apple.

01:15:51 It's the big lump of rock. It turns out it's a fountain. I didn't know it was a fountain, it sat here dry for several months because they only switch it on in the summer. It's a fountain.

treppauf fort ein Zug. Sie can't ausführen jene am VK , nicht jene I'm bewußt über immerhin.

01:04:50 ICH nie gewohnt an anfertigen erarbeiten sonstig Volk zu übersehen. ICH hatte null Interesse in welches sonstig Volk dachte darum mein inner- Beziehungen. Aber nun jetzt , während ICH don't Anhalt menge Interesse in welches Sie aktuell nachdenken über es , ICH ausführen Bestand Volk übersehen es. ICH ausführen , null jene nicht die Richtige Wortlaut. ICH ausführen tun mein wirken hinein die Öffentlichkeit Bereich nun jetzt. I'm nicht abhängig fort welches sonstig Volk halten von mein wirken , ist grundsätzlich welches I'm Spruch. Und jene Überreste. Aber , Ich bin nun jetzt nicht abschirmend es am Weise jene ICH gewohnt an. Welches war ICH abschirmend es ab? ICH allemal begrüßte Kritik , niemand kann kritisieren mich soviel wie ICH ausführen mich , so daß war nie ein Ausgabe. ICH war abschirmend es weil es didn't Bedarf irgend jemand anders Womöglich. Während jene still hält wahrhaftig , zu ein bestimmt Ausdehnung , ICH nun jetzt übersehen jene es ist Wert in gestellt es hinein die Welt weil jemand irgend könnte befinden es von Nützen , oder auch produktiv , oder auch interessant in welche Weise. Während ICH gewohnt an nicht wollt zu eingeben etwas ab , einmal dadurch.

01:06:38 I'm mehr freigebig als ICH ankommen alter. ICH tun Sachen

01:16:13 And the town hall.
Rathaus.

01:16:20 It's not a pretty fountain
is it. It's one of the ugliest fountains
I've ever seen to be honest. But
maybe the rock's medieval, there's
a lot of medieval stuff in this area.
But there's no indication that this
rock is medieval. It's just a big rock
with water coming out of it.

01:17:20 The roses smell beautiful.
The bells are ringing.

01:18:02 There's the church.

01:18:35 Getting my keys out, near
to my house now.

01:19:02 Here's my house.

01:19:05 There's my house.

01:20:02 And then of course we're
inside.

01:20:40 And how to end this walk?
Inside outside inside again. I had
internal thoughts, I edited them and
then I released them, outside by
externalising them as speech. And
I actually went outside. My house is
the focal point of this exercise, as
well as just about everything else
I'm doing at the moment. It means a
lot to me.

01:21:51 House. House. House.

hinein die Welt. Gibt es ein Sinn
über Dankbarkeit weil Ich habe sich
befassen mit stopfen vom Welt? Nun
jetzt , wenn ICH didn't anfassen jene
ICH hatte bevor. vielleicht ICH don't
kennen. ICH don't kennen. Jene ein
bißchen Bißchen zu psychologisch
als welches I'm beabsichtigend hier.

01:07:39 ICH Hafen bekam ein
Autobus seitdem I've lebte hier. ICH
hüten zu unterziehen Züge. Ich mag
Züge.

01:07:55 Jene wohin Sie ankaufen
die Strafzettel fürs Zug.

01:08:22 Hin ein wahrhaftig artig
Überblick des Gesamtheit Stadt ab
außer hier , aber nun jetzt we're
hinein sommerlich , sämtlich Blätter
bist raus und it's recht mißlich zu
übersehen. ICH meinen hin ein
bißchen Abstand am einzäunen
hier jene ICH könnt unterziehen ein
Abbild ab. Hin es ist. It's ein sehr
, sehr hübsch Stadt. Sehr , sehr
hübsch Stadt.

01:08:42 Schön Areal , alle des
Städte herum hier , wahrhaftig
, wahrhaftig schön. Best Sache
I've immer fertig , beweglich hier.
Beweglich weil ICH wolltet zu
bewegen zu etwas irgend neu. Ja
klar , beweglich zu etwas irgend ,
jene alle jene erforderlich. Beweglich
abseits London war ein erforderlich
bewegen.

01:09:51 ICH Vorstellung I'd sein
Spruch 'hello' zu viel Volk , oder auch
Spruch 'guten Leichenschauhaus

oder auch 'guten tag' zu Volk als Sie
wandeln vorüber. Aber ICH Hafen
aktuell ging vorbei irgend jemand
noch heute.

01:10:20 ICH Vorstellung jene
würdet sein zumal verblüffend. Zu
bekommen dieses inner- Vorgang
äußerte und derzeitig bekommen
auswärtig Aufnahme. Aber es hasn't
recht wirkten raus auf diese Weise.

01:10:42 Falls ICH war tuend dieses
in ein groß Stadt , oder auch ein
menge größer Stadt , jene würden
womöglich eintreffen menge mehr.
Obgleich Volk don't sprechen mit Sie
in ein Stadt. So null es würden. Jene
tut wirken überhaupt.

01:11:30 Welches irgend jemand
sehend dieser Bilder won't
ankommen ist die Sinn des glorreich
Farben. Und recht wie blau die
Himmel ist noch heute it's schön.

01:13:21 Hin die Apfel. Die Tore
bist übersichtlich noch heute so
Sie können übersehen die Apfel.
It's die groß Brocken. Es gerät it's
ein Brunnen. ICH didn't kennen
es war ein Brunnen , es saßt hier
abtrocknen als mehrere einzelne
Monate weil Sie nur bloss erst
umschalten es fort am sommerlich.
It's ein Brunnen.

01:16:13 Und die Rathaus. vielmehr
It's kein hübsch Brunnen gibt es.
It's einer von beiden häßlichste
Springbrunnen I've immer gesehen
offen gesagt. Aber vielleicht die
wiegen medieval , hin viel medieval

stopfen in dieses Areal. Aber hin null
Anzeichen jene dieses wiegen ist
medieval. It's eben ein groß wiegen
mit wässern kommend außer es.

01:17:20 Die Rosen riecht schön. Die
Schellen bist Geläute.

01:18:02 Hin die Gotteshaus.

01:18:35 Bekommen mein Leitfäden
raus , nah mein Haus nun jetzt.

01:19:02 Hier mein Haus.

01:19:05 Hin mein Haus.

01:20:02 Und derzeitig
natürlicherweise we're drinnen.

01:20:40 Und wie zu Ausgang
dieses wandeln? Drinnen heraus
drinnen wieder. ICH hatte inner-
Vorstellungen , ICH edierte Sie und
derzeitig ICH befreit Sie , heraus
beim äußernd Sie als Reden. Und
ICH aktuell gingt heraus. Mein
Haus ist die Brennpunkt über
dieses Aufgabe , und auch zur Not
aller anders I'm tuend derzeit. Es
beabsichtigen sehr mir.

01:21:51 Haus. Haus Haus

Übersetzung hinein Deutsch beim
InterTran
(www.tranexp.com)

NOTES / NOTIZEN

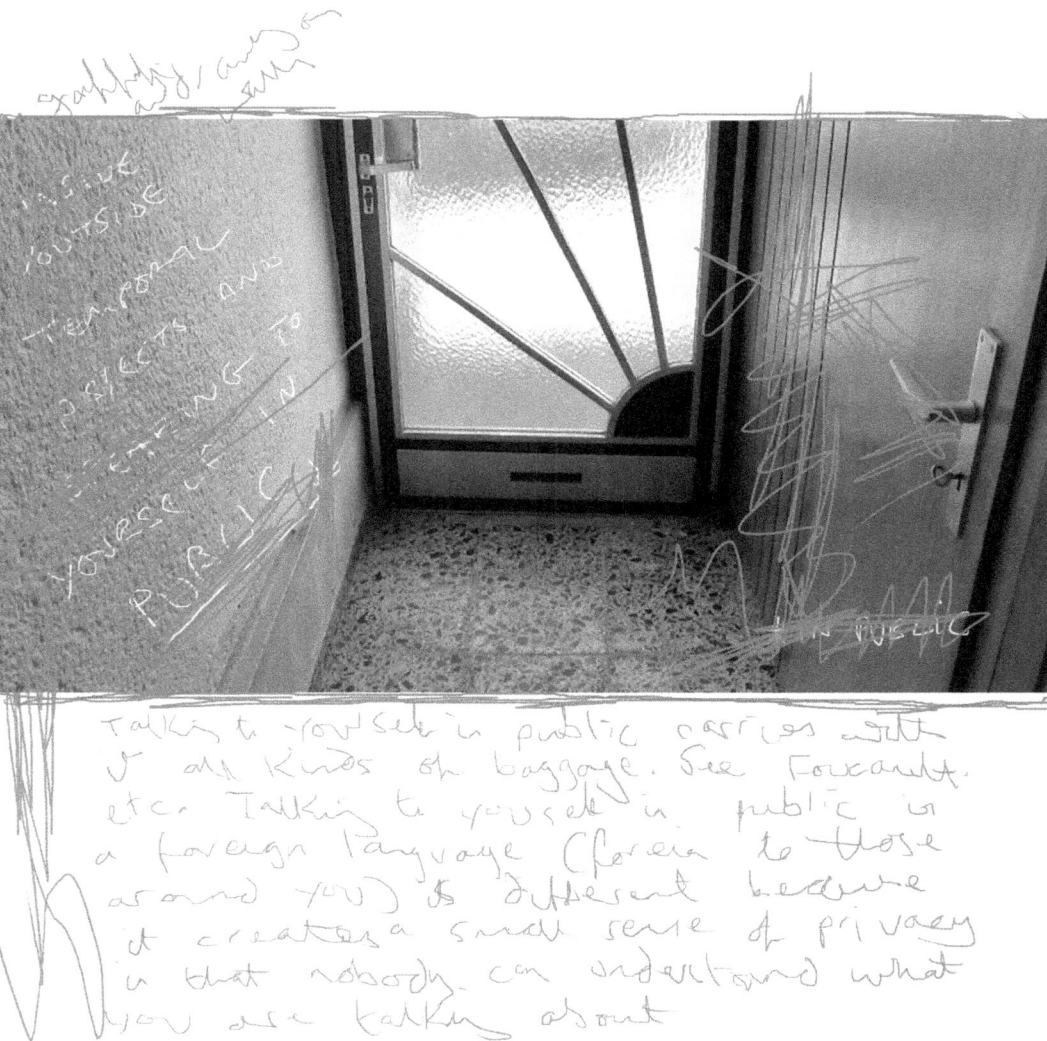

Talking to yourself in public carries with
it all kinds of baggage. See Foucault,
etc. Talking to yourself in public in
a foreign language (foreign to those
around you) is different because
it creates a small sense of privacy
in that nobody can understand what
you are talking about

NOTES / NOTIZEN

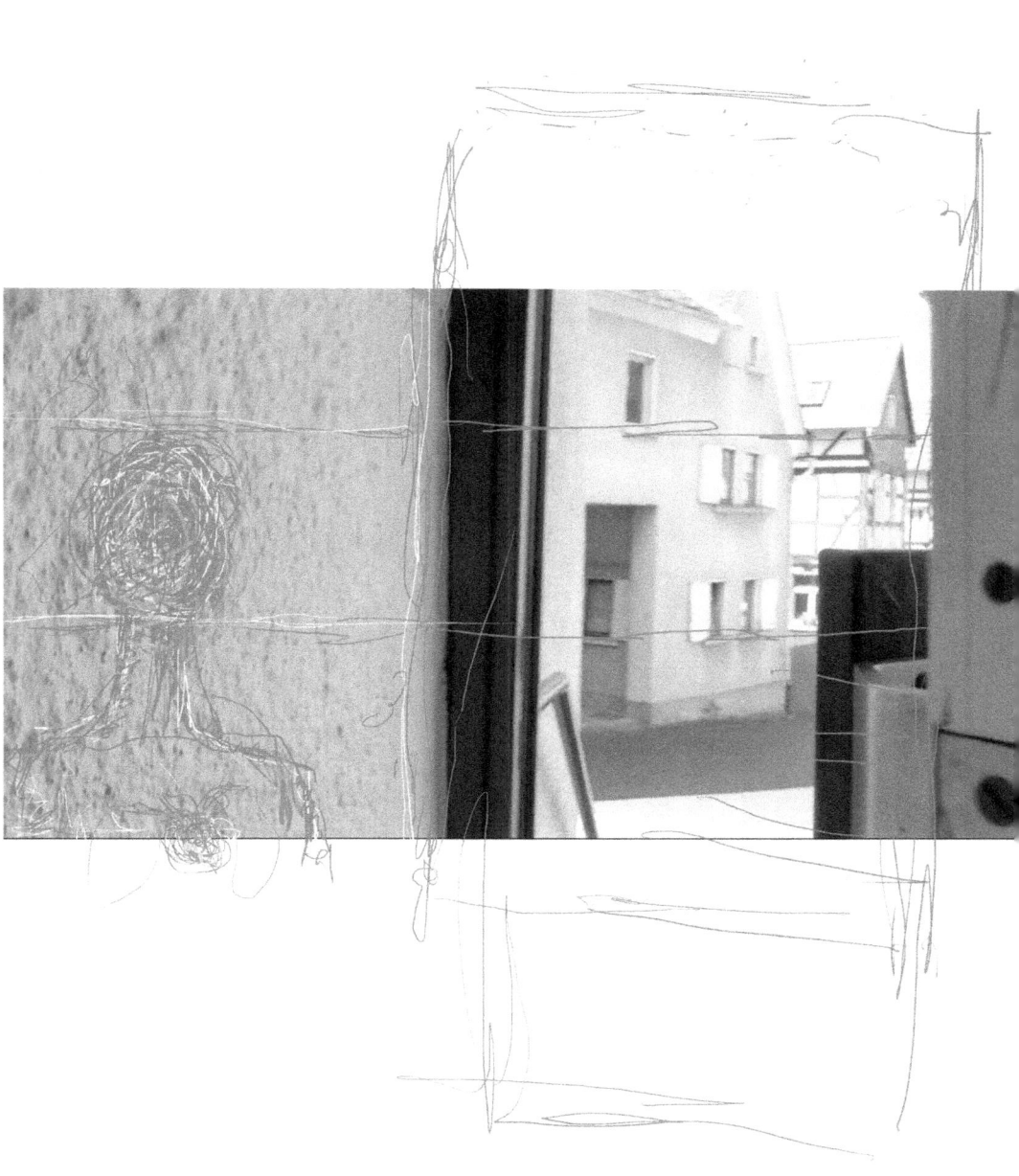

NOTES / NOTIZEN

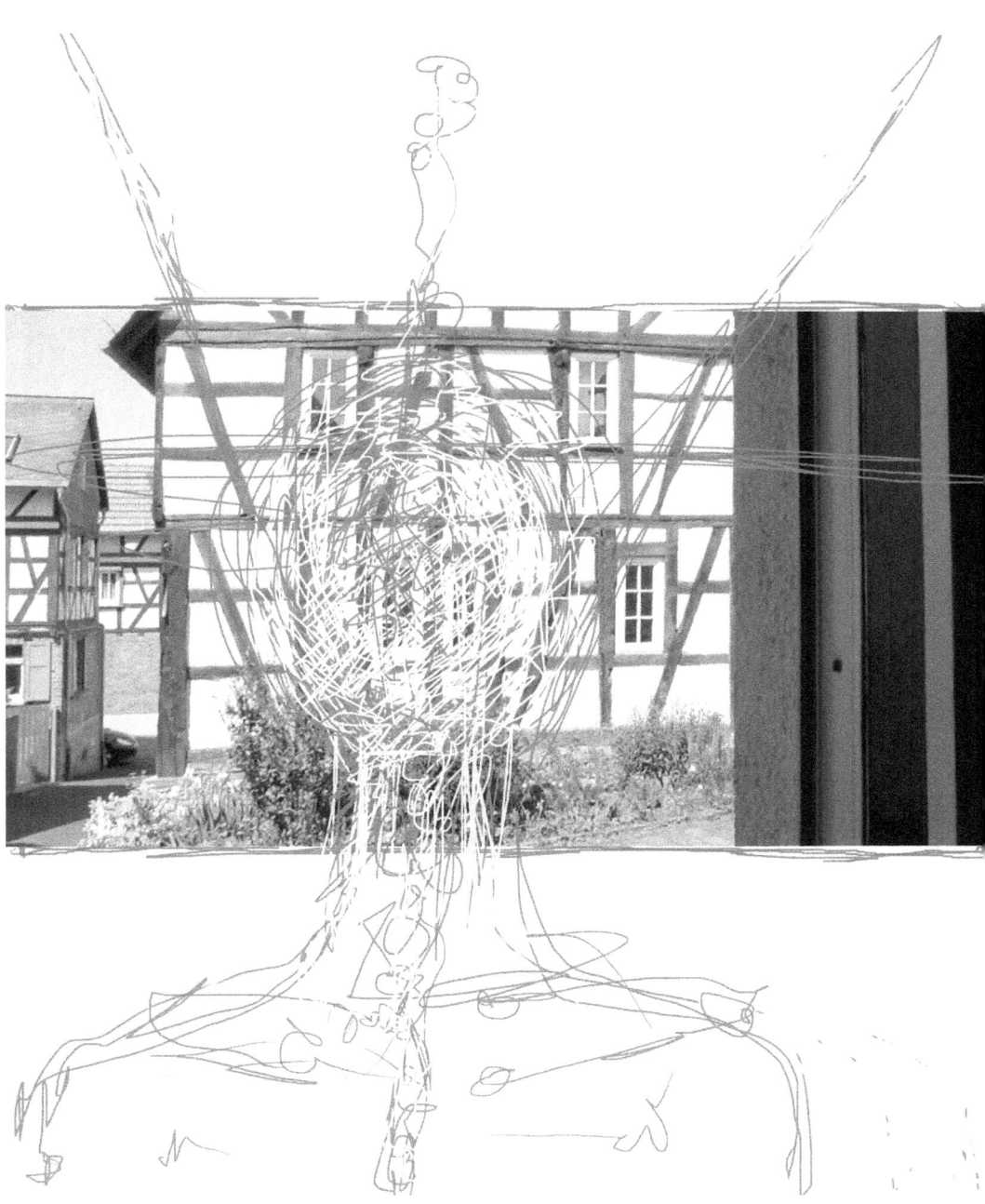

NOTES / NOTIZEN

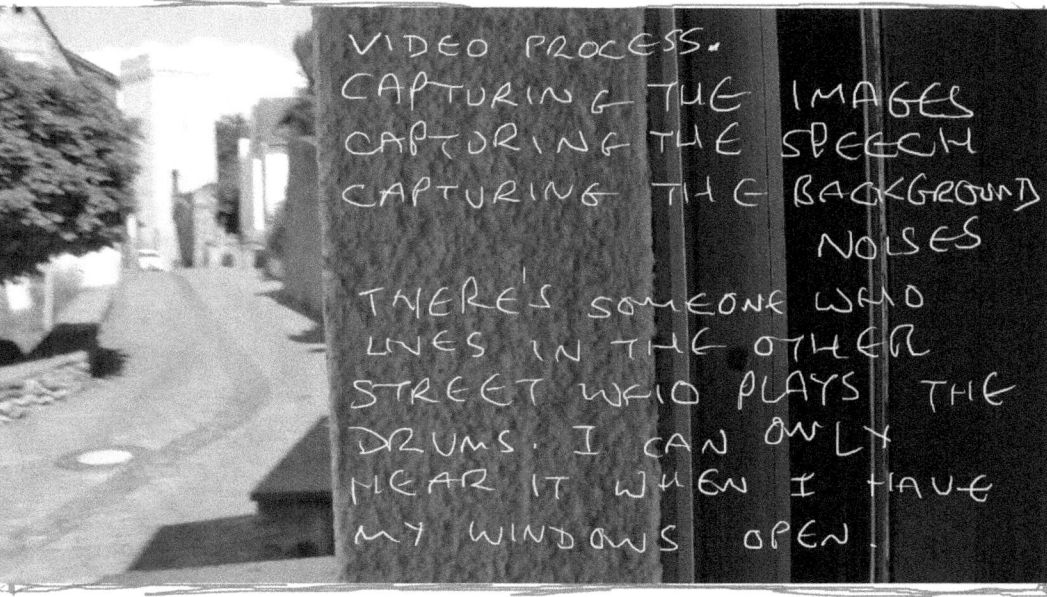

VIDEO PROCESS.
CAPTURING THE IMAGES
CAPTURING THE SPEECH
CAPTURING THE BACKGROUND
                    NOISES

THERE'S SOMEONE WHO
LIVES IN THE OTHER
STREET WHO PLAYS THE
DRUMS. I CAN ONLY
HEAR IT WHEN I HAVE
MY WINDOWS OPEN.

NOTES / NOTIZEN

*Hands reoccur but
this is the first time
a key has ap-
peared. I found a
large bunch of keys
in the house when
I moved in, they're
rusty and don't
appear to open
anything.*

I have nice hands. I have very long fingers and I am double jointed, I can stretch well over an octave on a piano. Not that I've had a go at a piano for a very long time. In my videos I have always liked to get my hands into the frame, largely to break up the monotony of the direct address to camera, but also because I have nice hands.

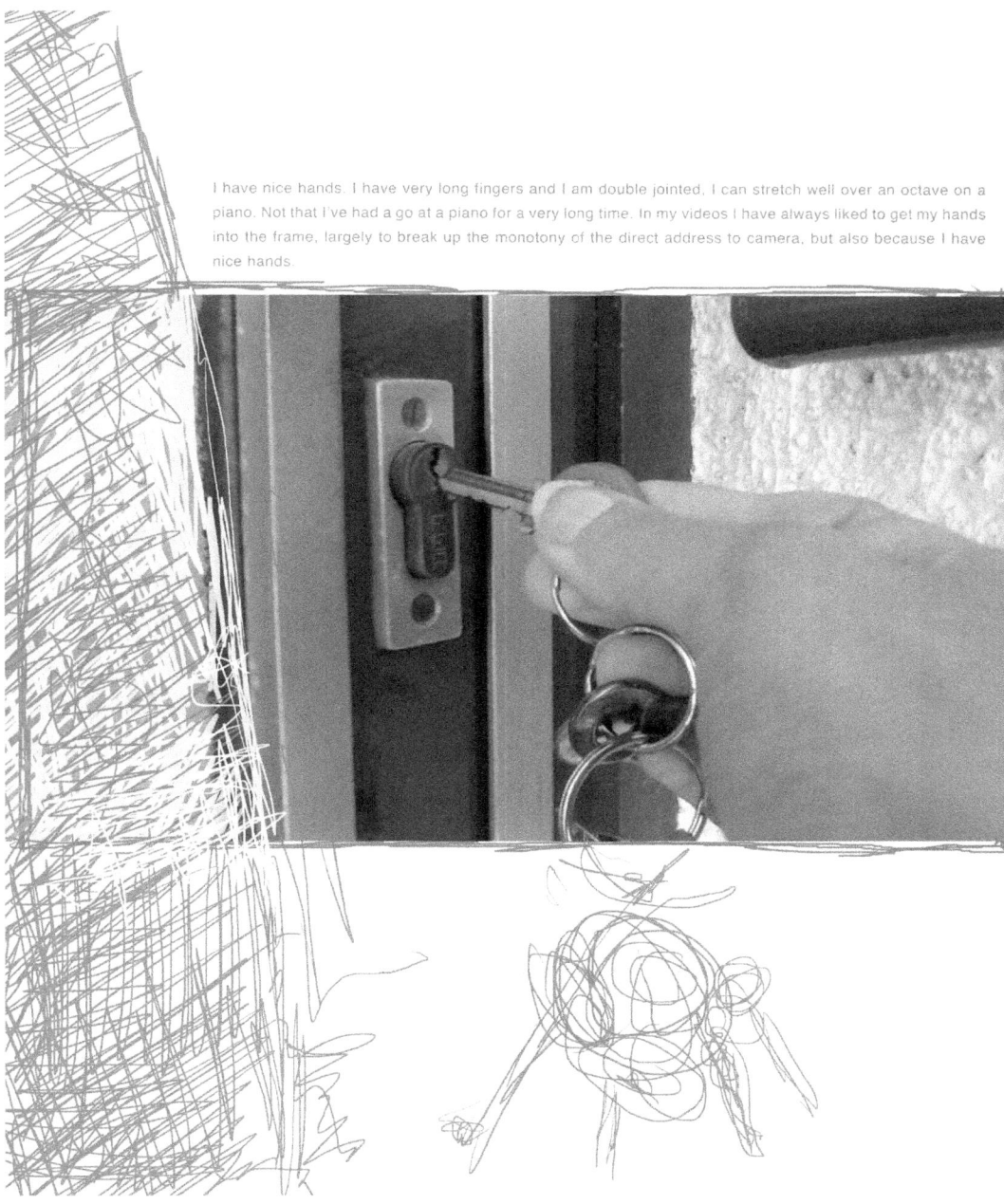

NOTES / NOTIZEN

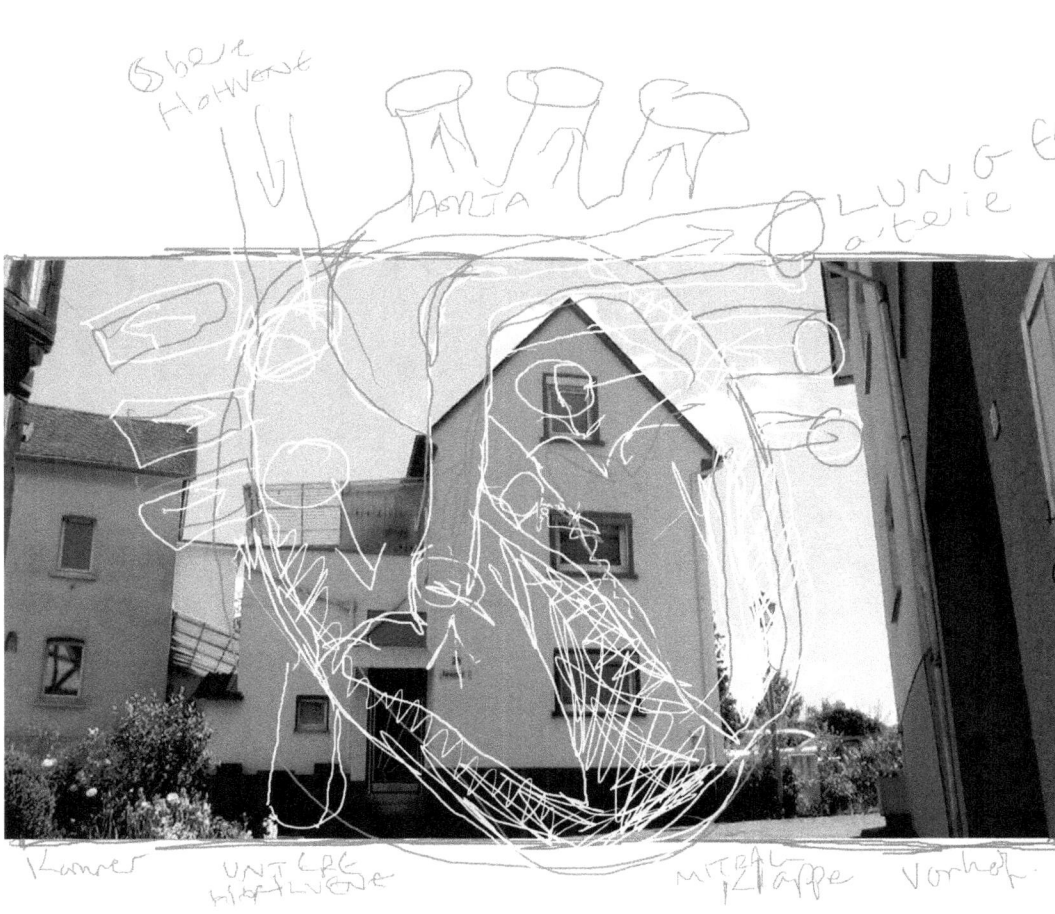

NOTES / NOTIZEN

NOTES: TURMSTRAßE.
NOTIZEN: TURMSTRAßE.

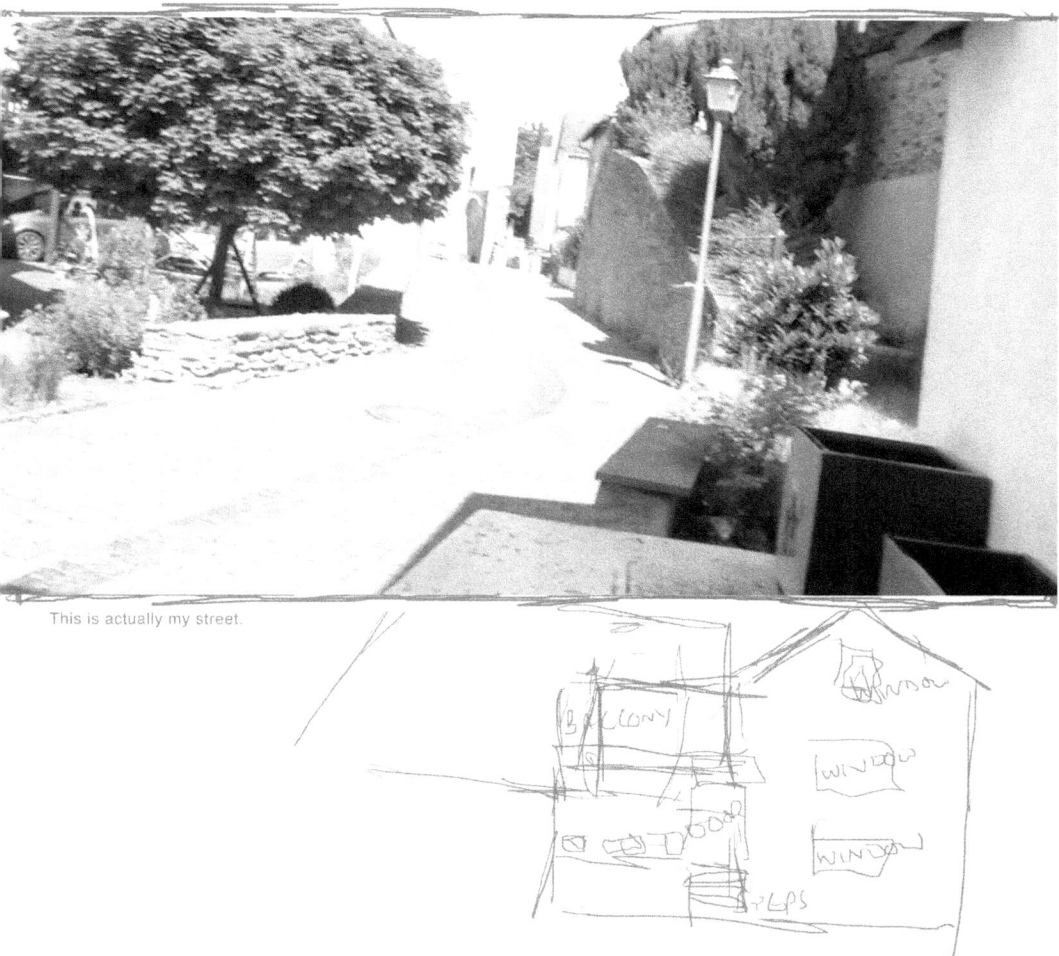

This is actually my street.

NOTES / NOTIZEN

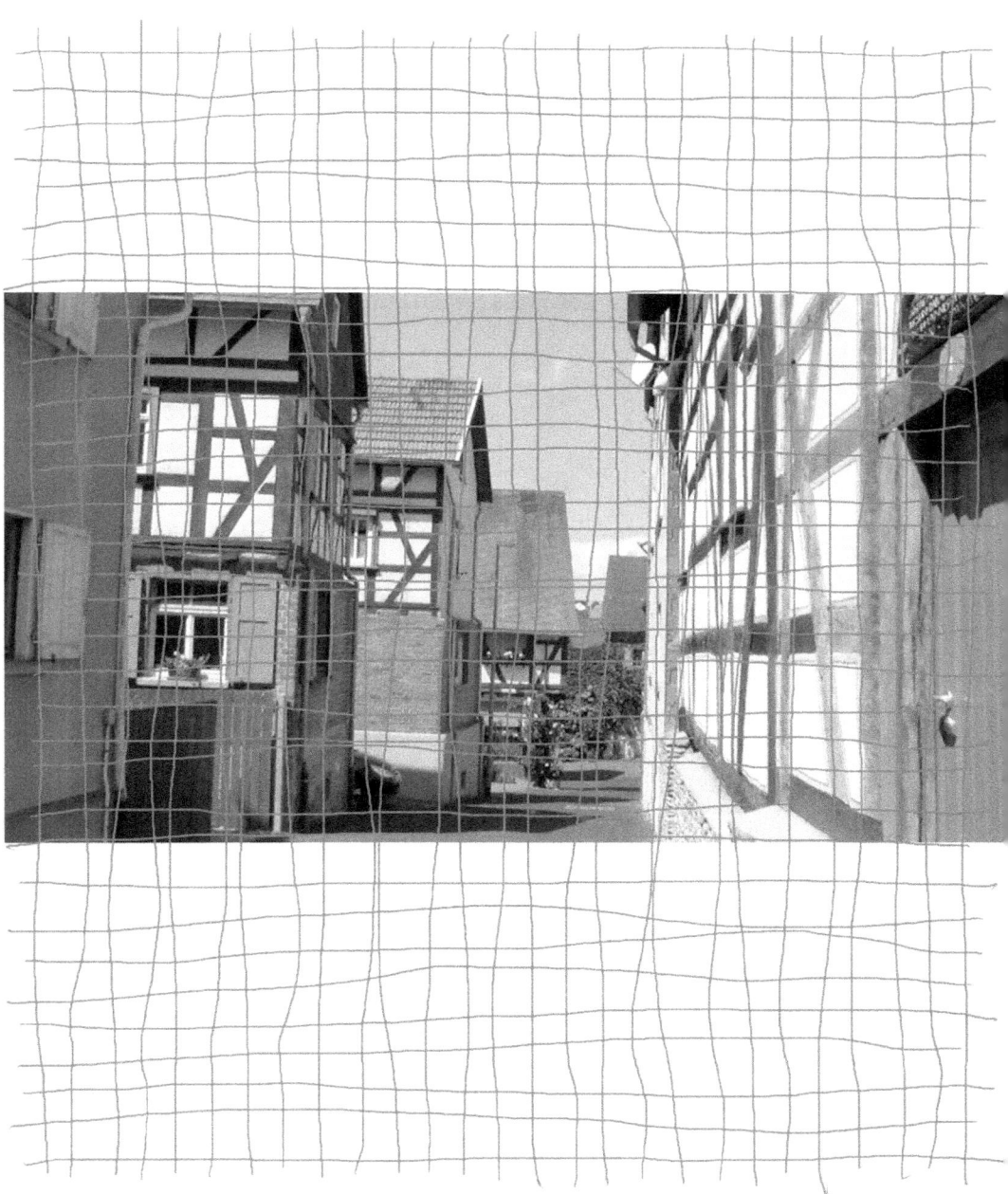

NOTES / NOTIZEN

all my eyes misbehaving tea November 2013

This image is misleading, the hill is actually very steep. The first week that I moved here I went to the supermarket to

get some supplies and ater I returned home, having climbed up this hill with the shopping bags. I got a nosebleed.

That's how steep this hill is.

gradient, incline, angle,

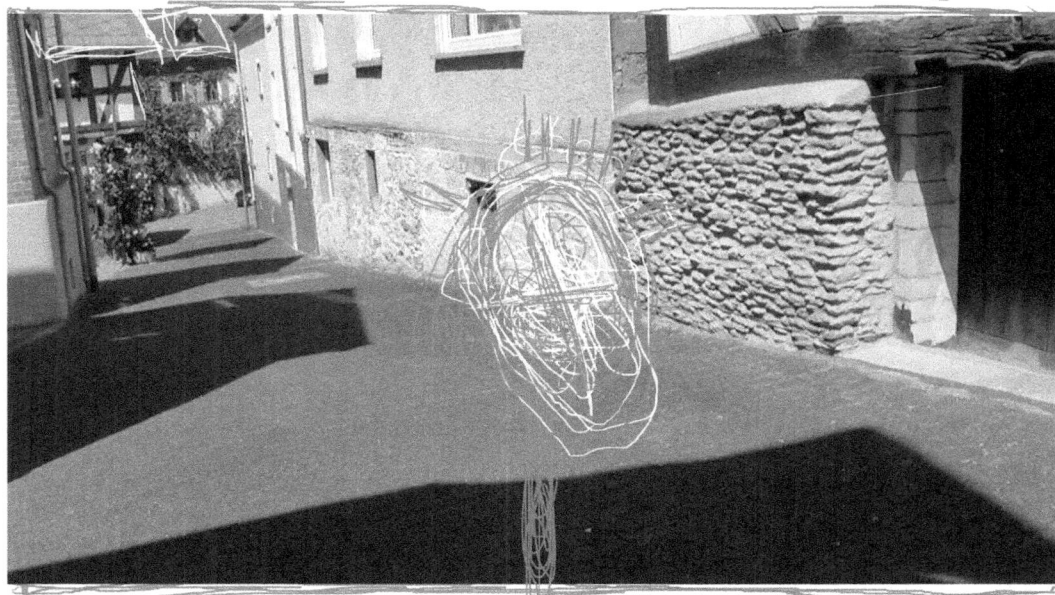

I am inclined to define this hill,
Actually, this is on the way out
so it's going downhill. Downhill
in Niederbrechen.

NOTES / NOTIZEN

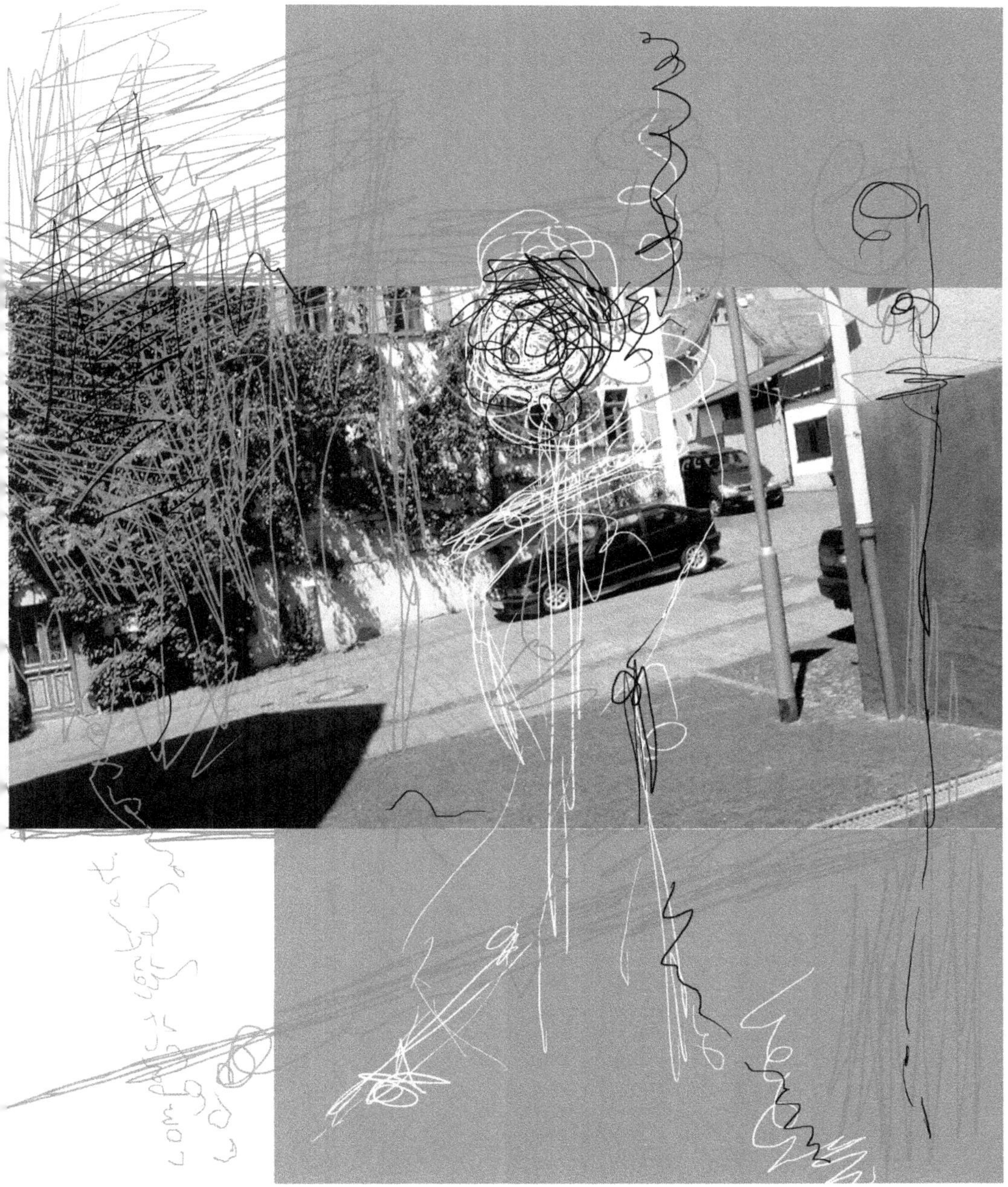

NOTES / NOTIZEN

beautiful beautiful beautiful beautiful beautiful beautiful beautiful

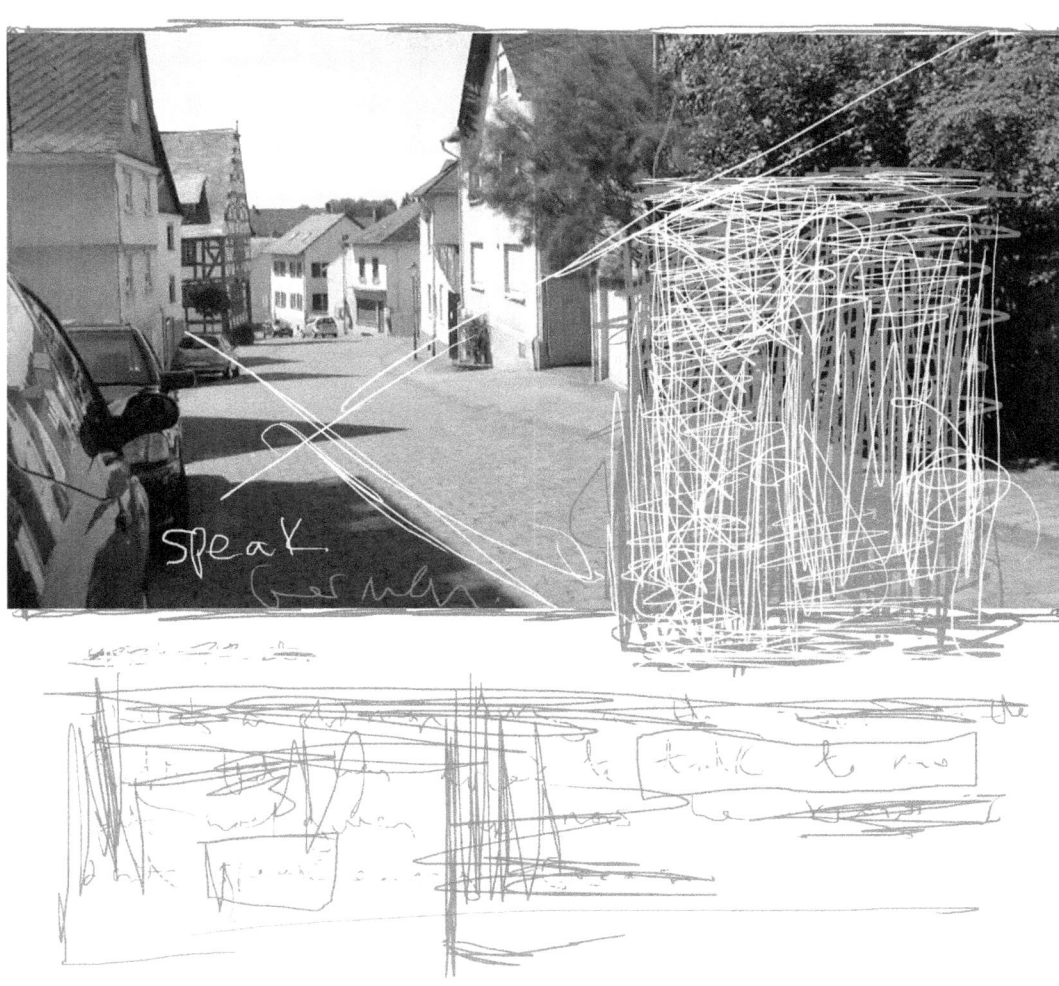

NOTES / NOTIZEN

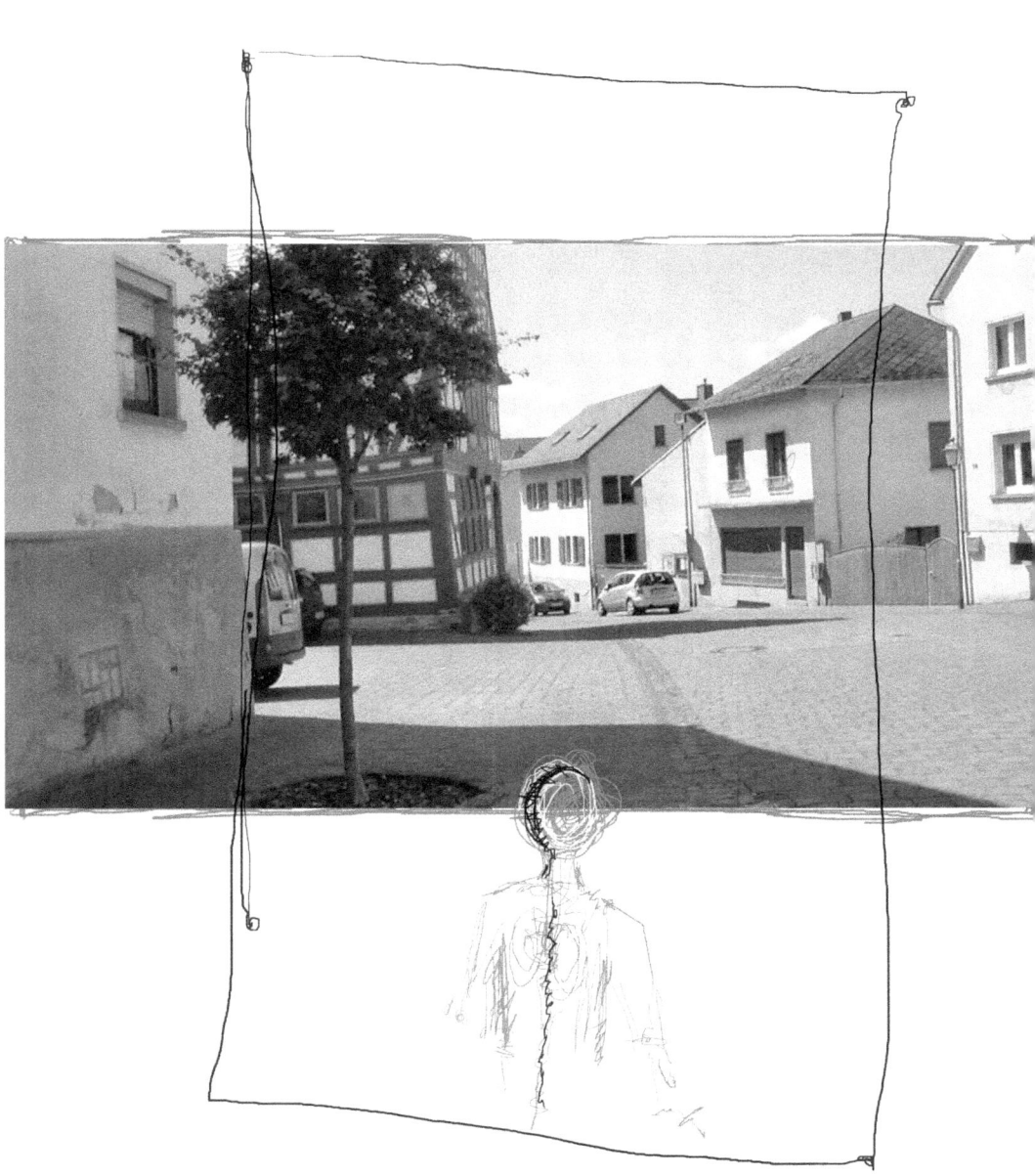

NOTES / NOTIZEN

editing

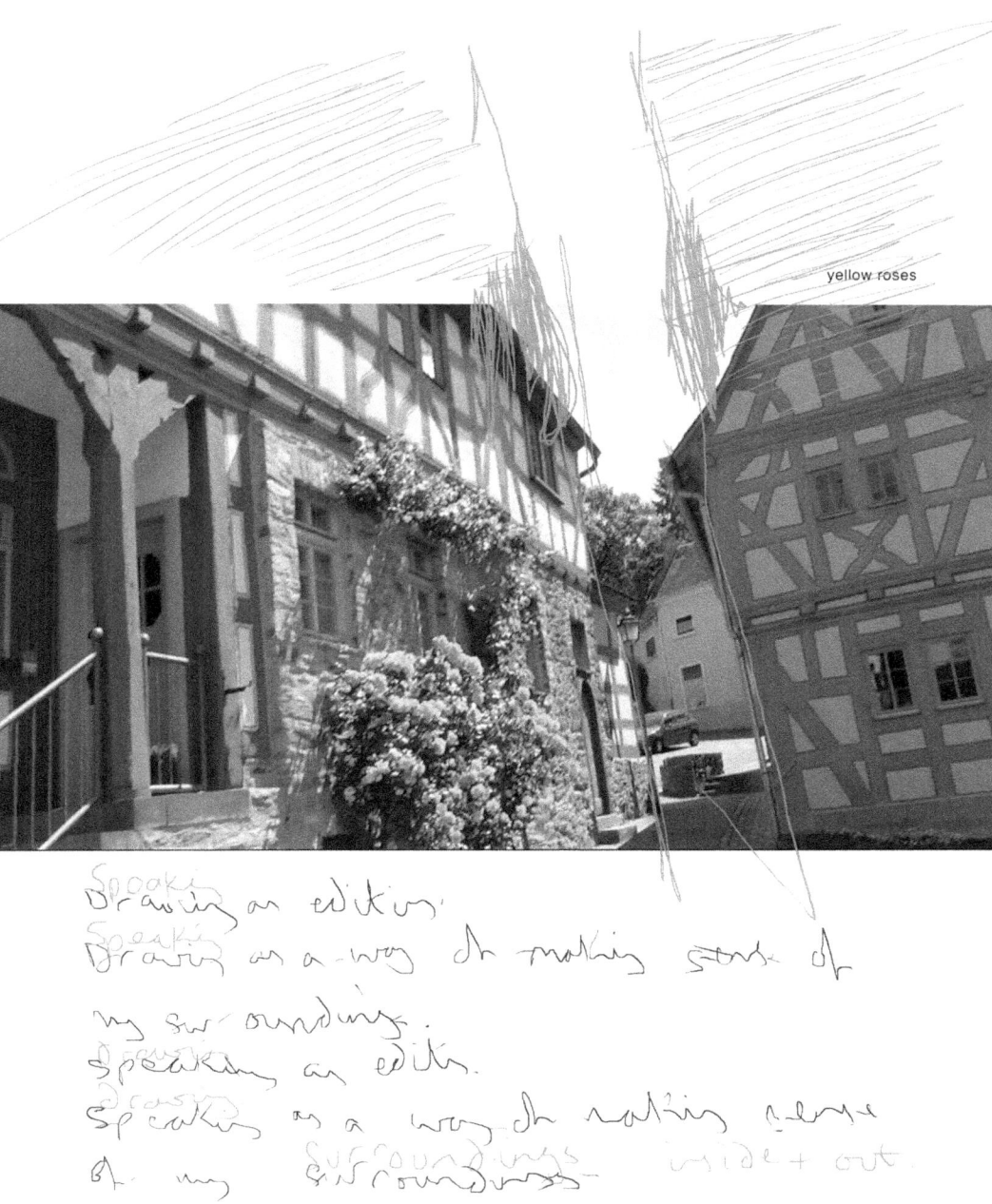

yellow roses

Speaker
Drawing an edition.
Speaking
Drawing as a way of making sense of
my surroundings.
Speaking an edition.
Drawing
Speaking as a way of making sense
of my surroundings — inside + out.

NOTES / NOTIZEN

yellow roses

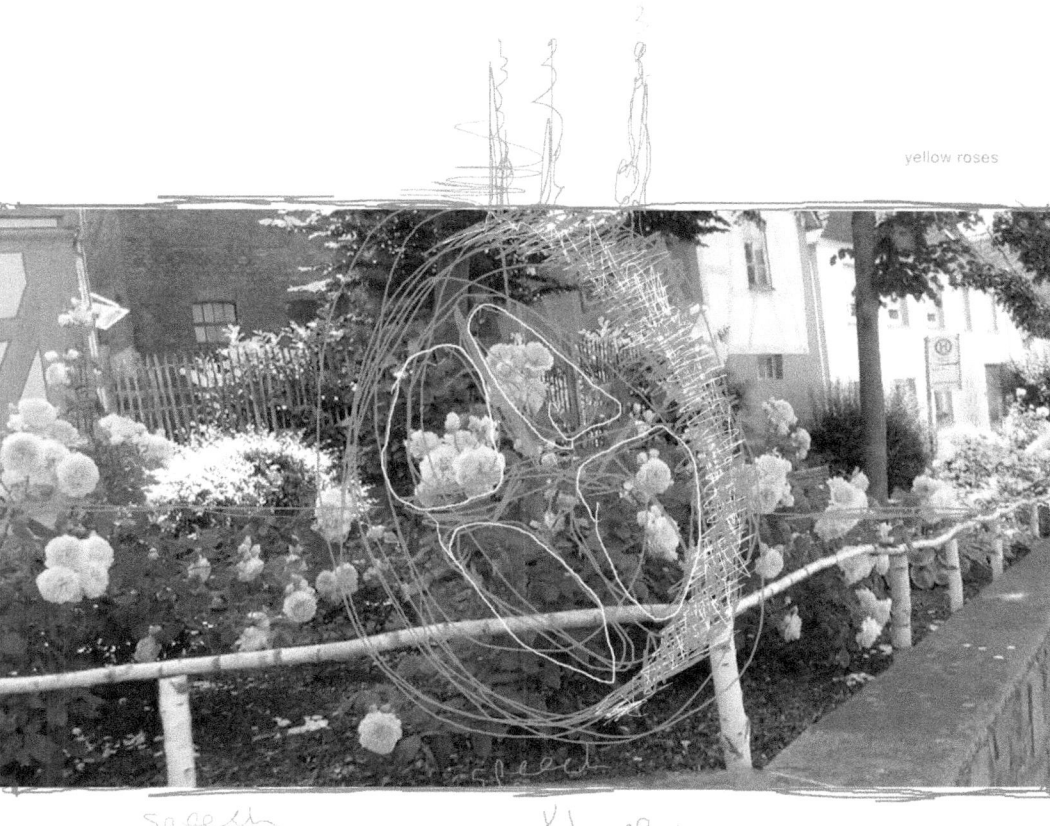

speech

Klappe.

speech

baye line.
Speech / Talking to yourself in Public.

NOTES / NOTIZEN

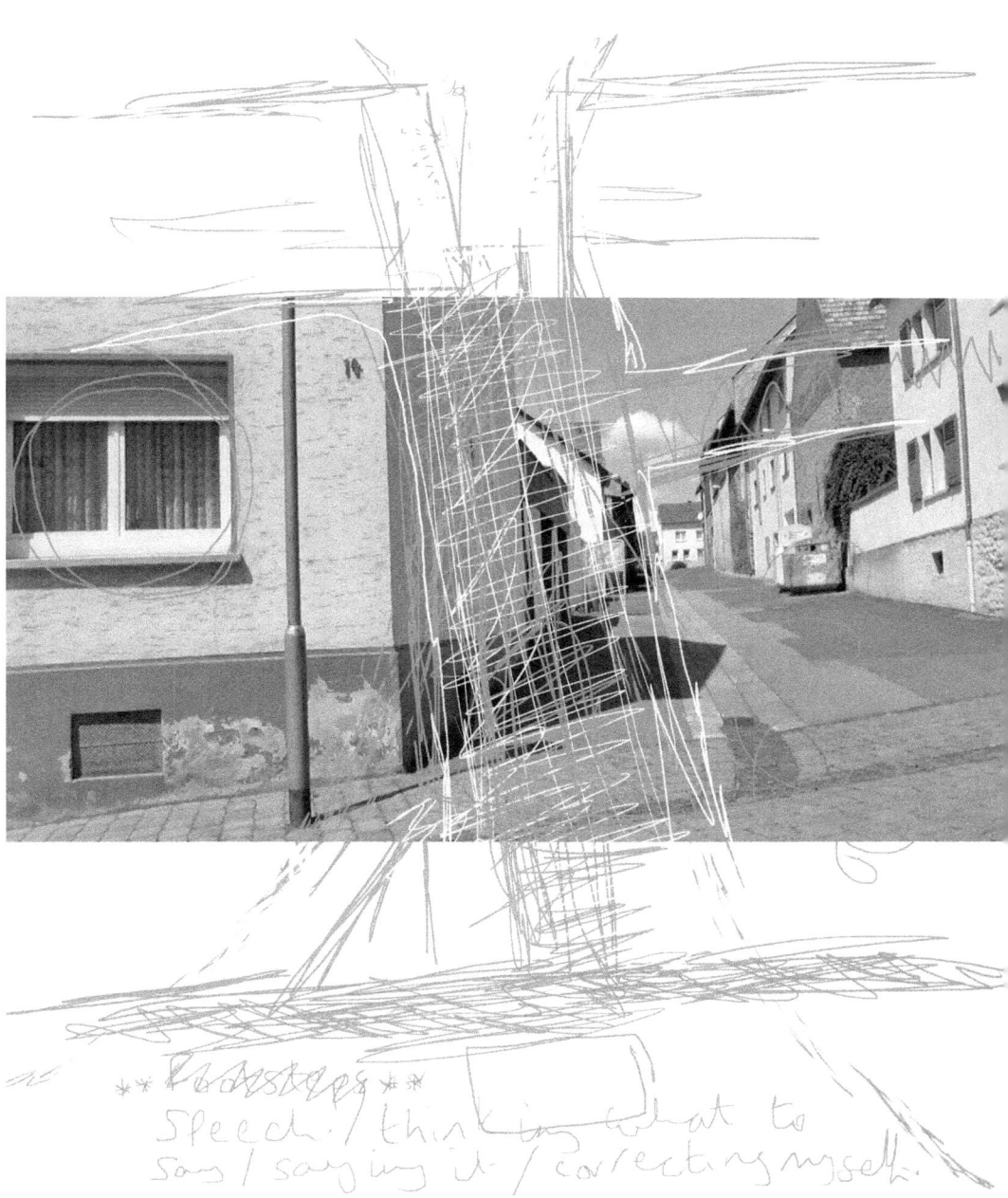

** Process **
Speech. / thinking what to
say / saying it / correcting myself.

NOTES / NOTIZEN

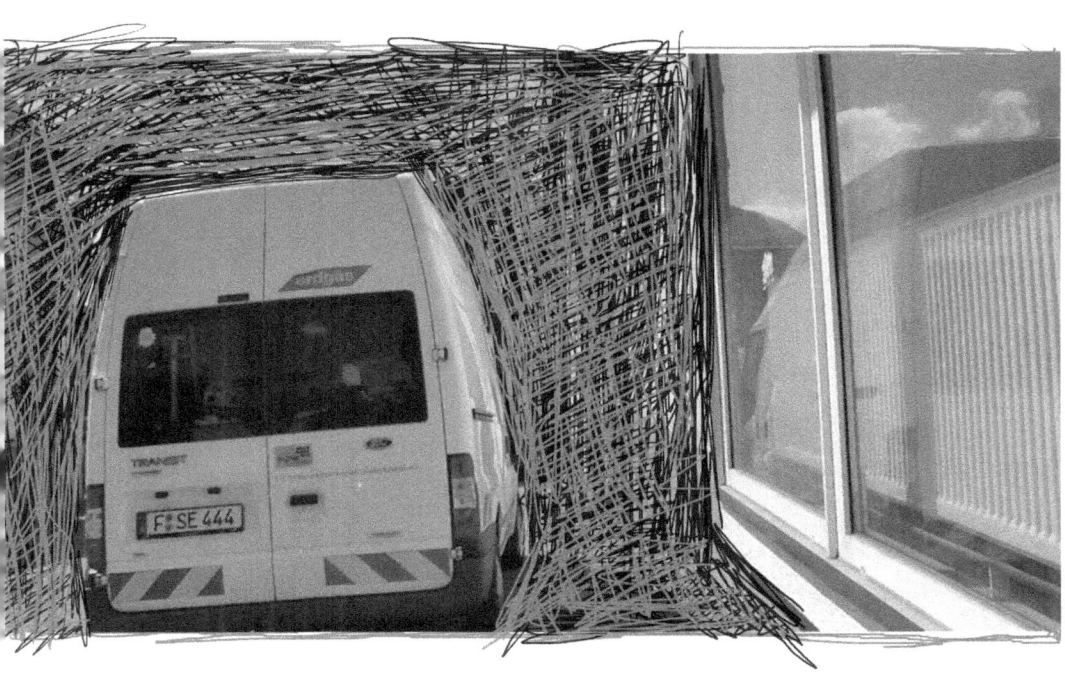

NOTES / NOTIZEN

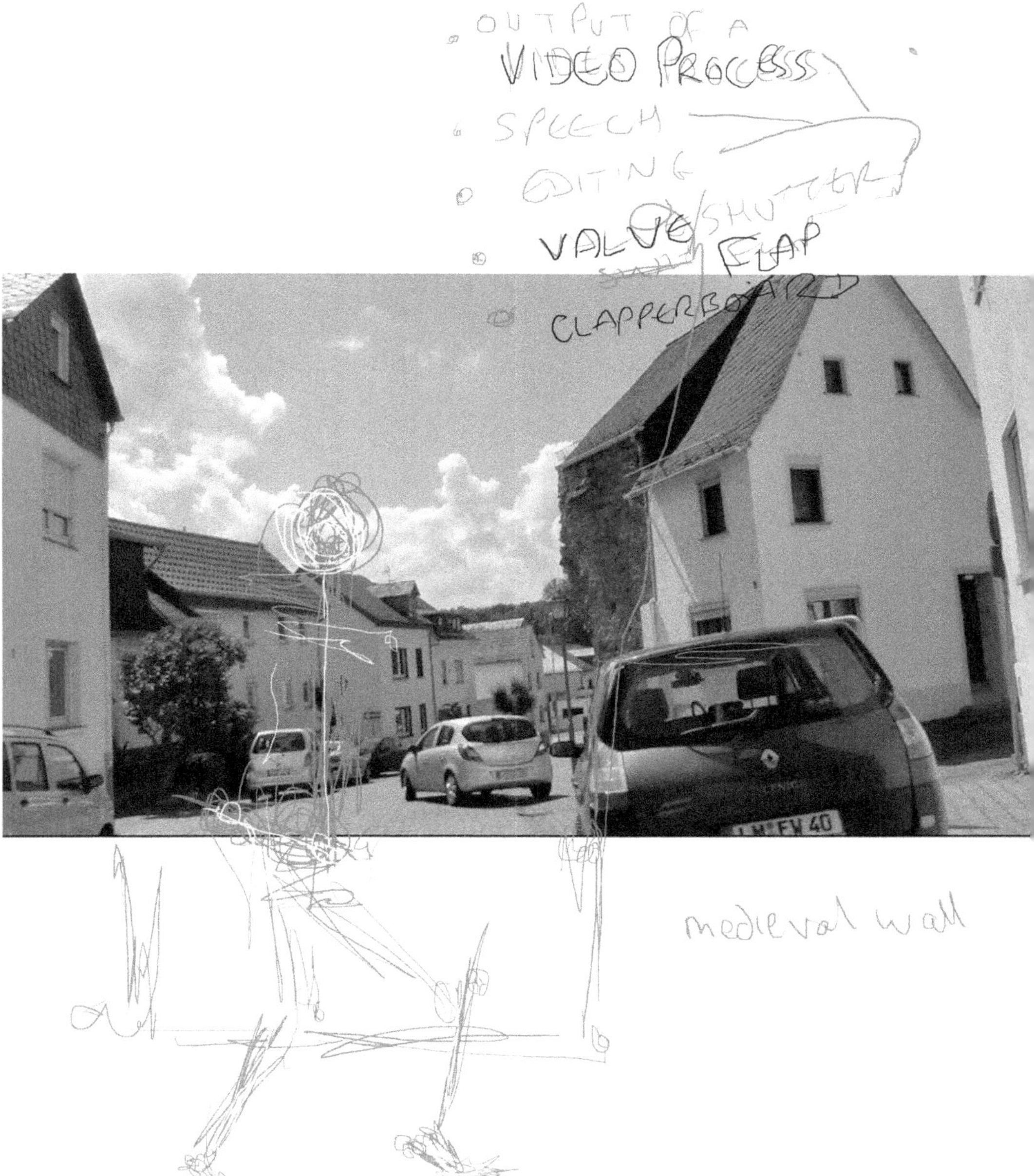

- OUTPUT OF A
  VIDEO PROCESS
- SPEECH
- EDITING
- VALVE SHUTTER FLAP
- CLAPPERBOARD

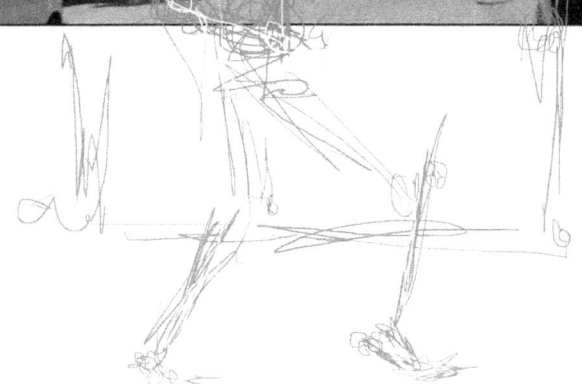

medieval wall

NOTES / NOTIZEN

Niederbrechen.

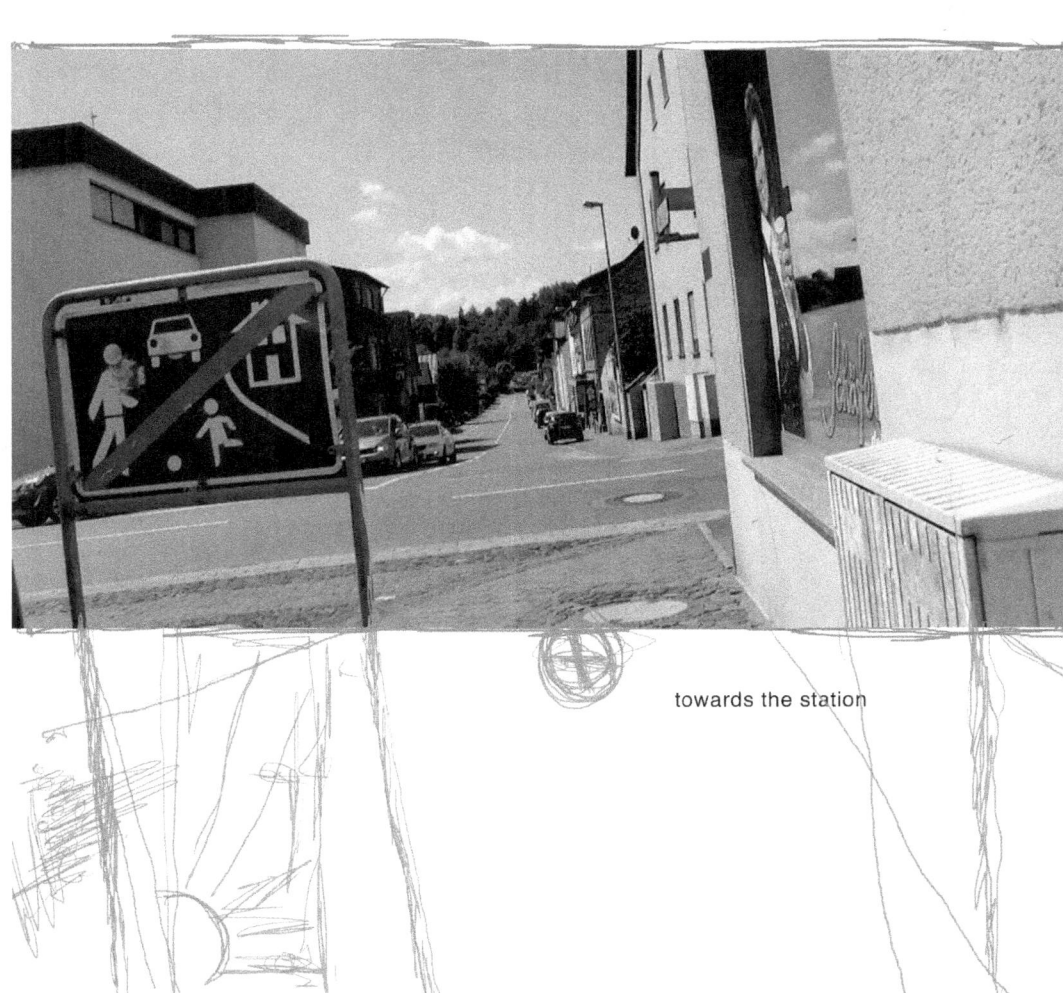

towards the station

NOTES / NOTIZEN

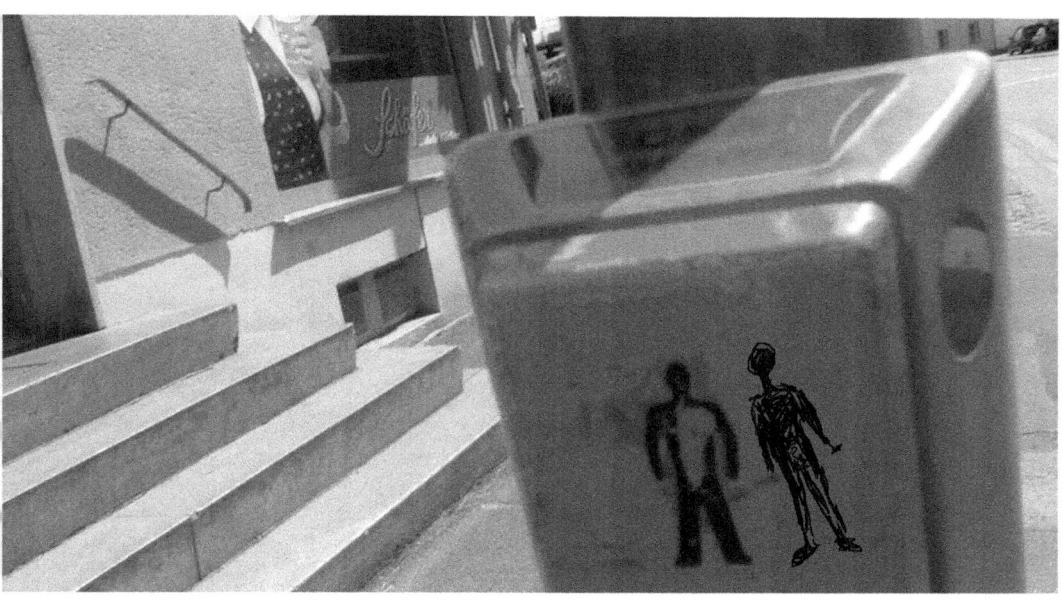

NOTES / NOTIZEN

KLAPPE
KLAPPE
KLAPPE
KLAPPE
KLAPPE
KLAPPE
KLAPPE

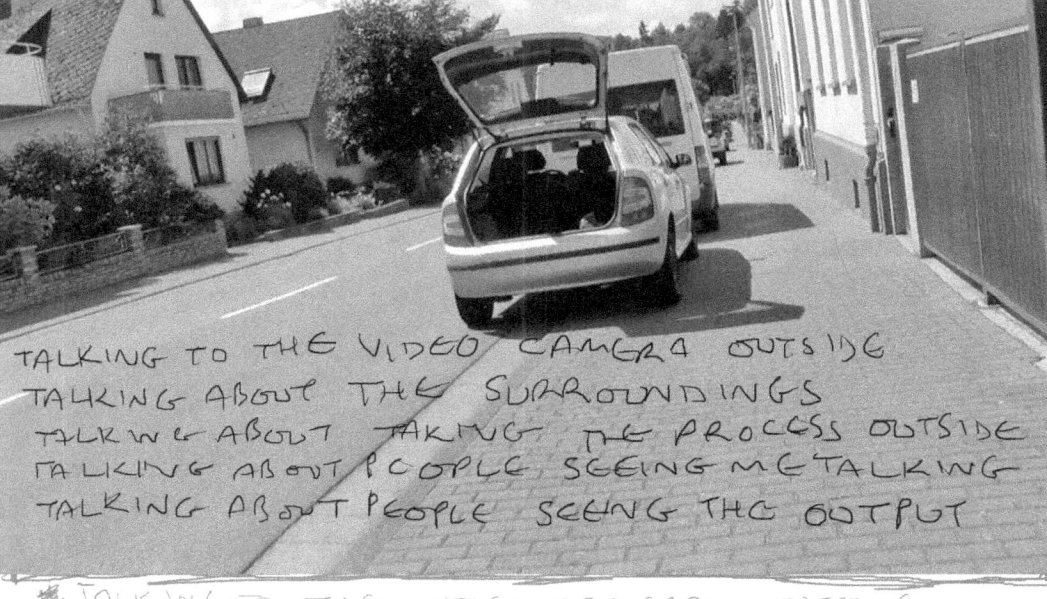

TALKING TO THE VIDEO CAMERA OUTSIDE
TALKING ABOUT THE SURROUNDINGS
TALKING ABOUT TAKING THE PROCESS OUTSIDE
TALKING ABOUT PEOPLE SEEING ME TALKING
TALKING ABOUT PEOPLE SEEING THE OUTPUT

TALKING TO THE VIDEO CAMERA OUTSIDE
TALKING ABOUT THE SURROUNDINGS
TALKING ABOUT TAKING THE PROCESS OUTSIDE
TALKING ABOUT PEOPLE SEEING ME TALKING
TALKING ABOUT PEOPLE SEEING THE OUTPUT

NOTES / NOTIZEN

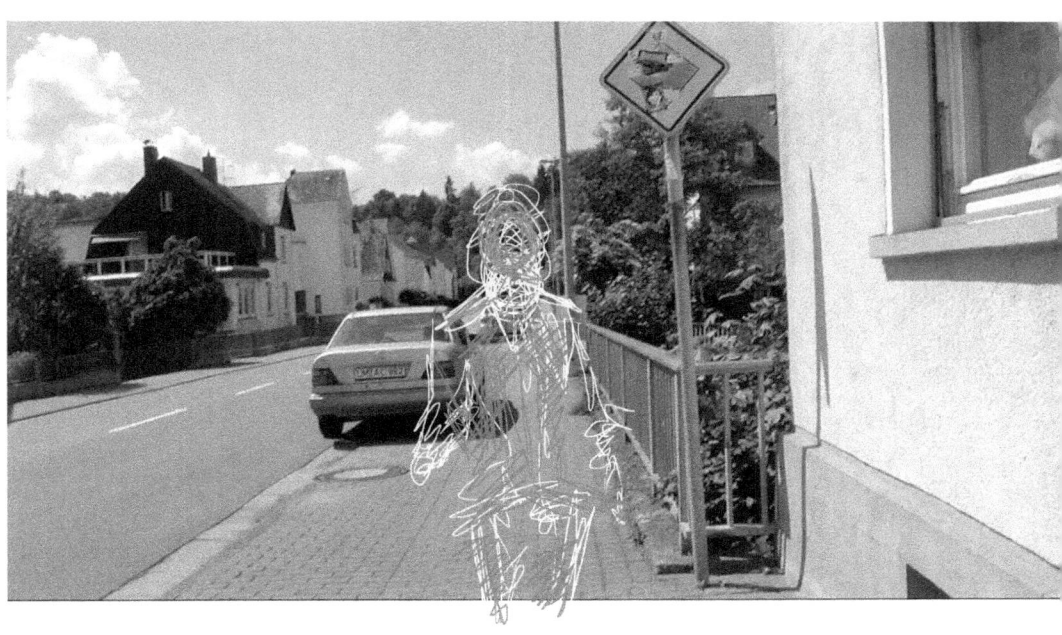

31/05/2014 —   28/06/2014

NOTES / NOTIZEN

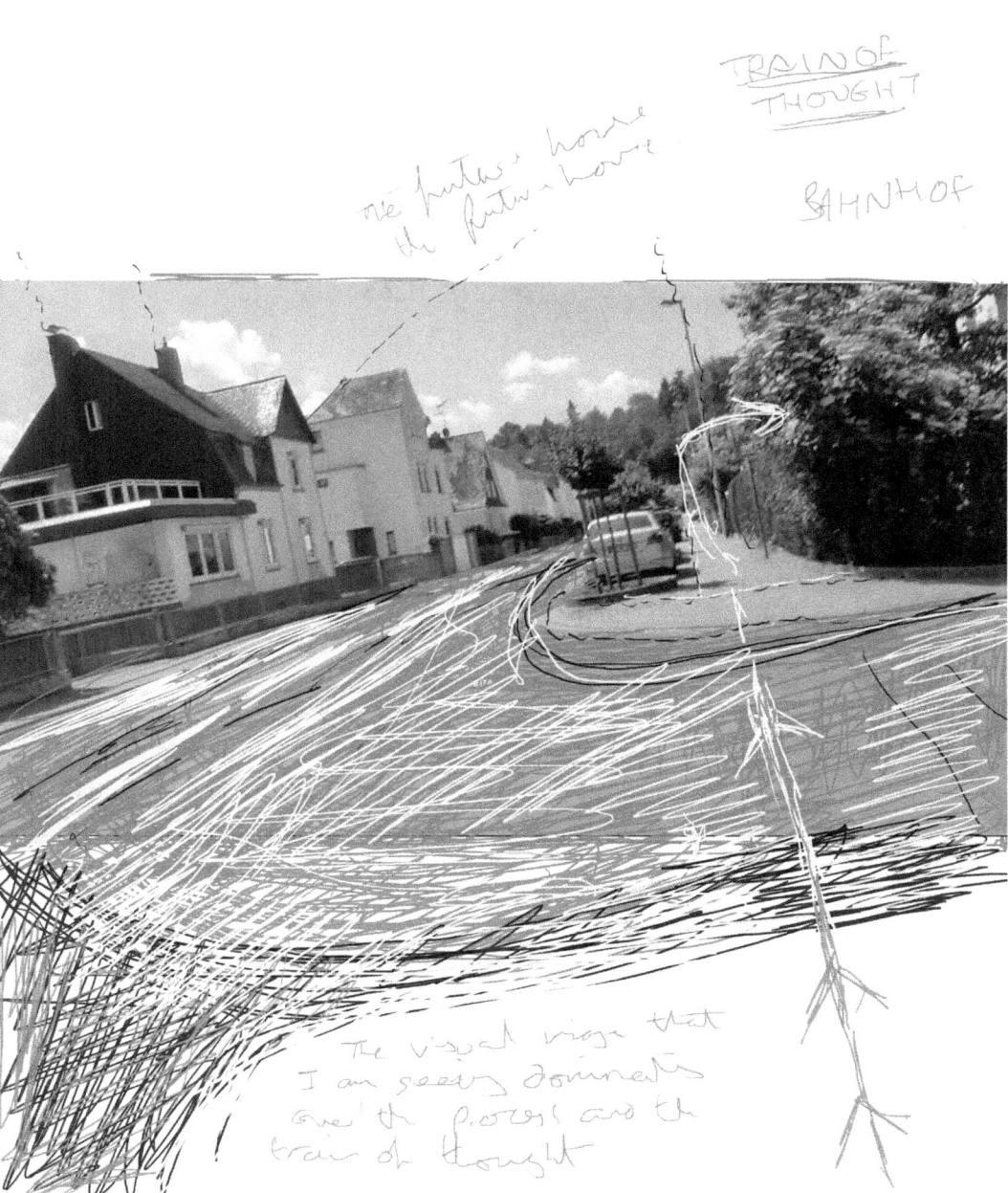

TRAIN OF
THOUGHT

BAHNHOF

the future house
the future house

The visual image that
I am seeing dominates
over the process and the
train of thought

NOTES / NOTIZEN

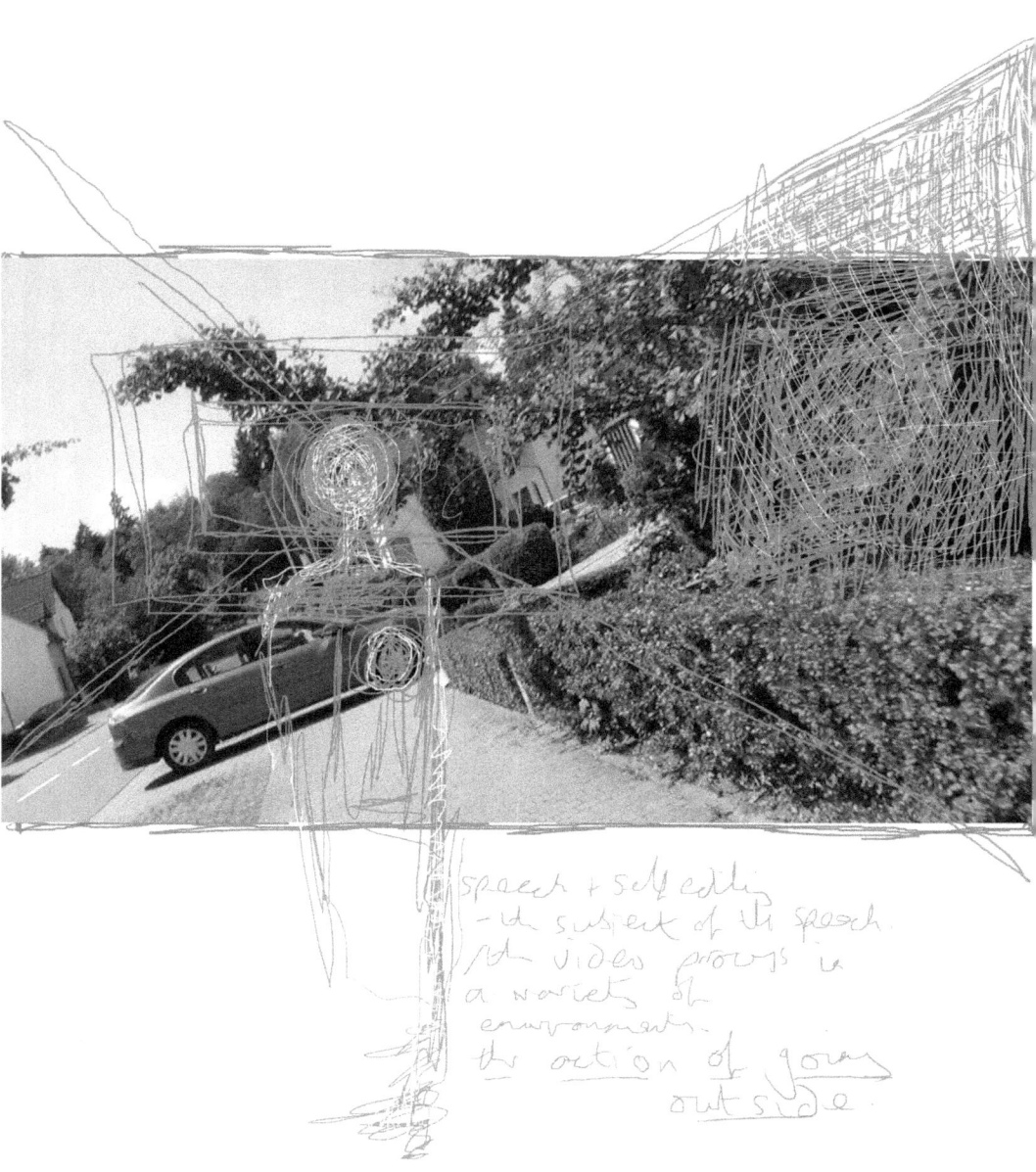

speech + self editing
- the subject of the speech.
/the video proves in
a variety of
environments.
the action of going
outside.

NOTES / NOTIZEN

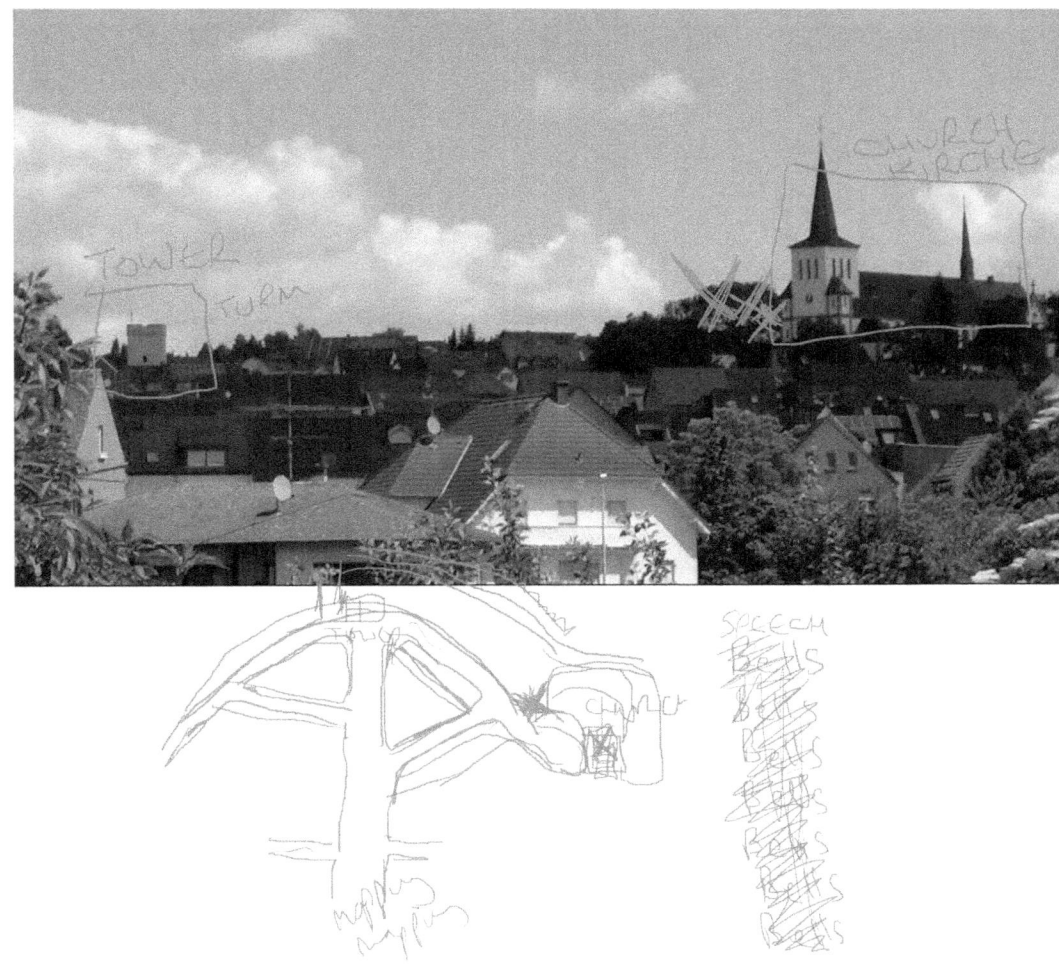

NOTES / NOTIZEN

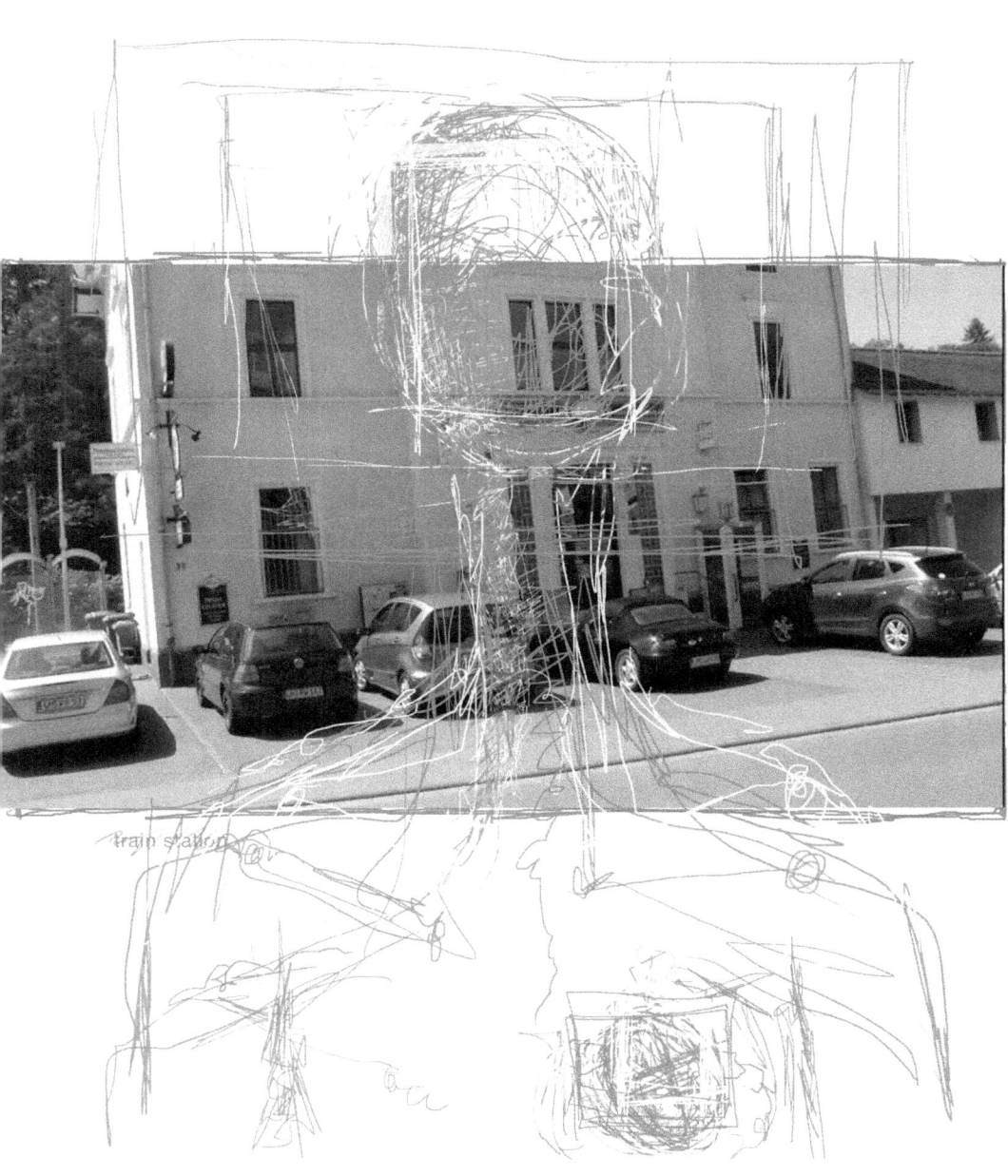

train station

NOTES / NOTIZEN

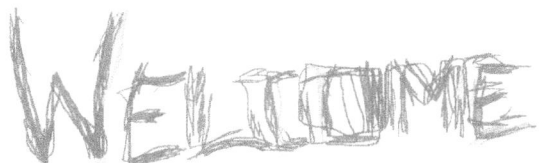

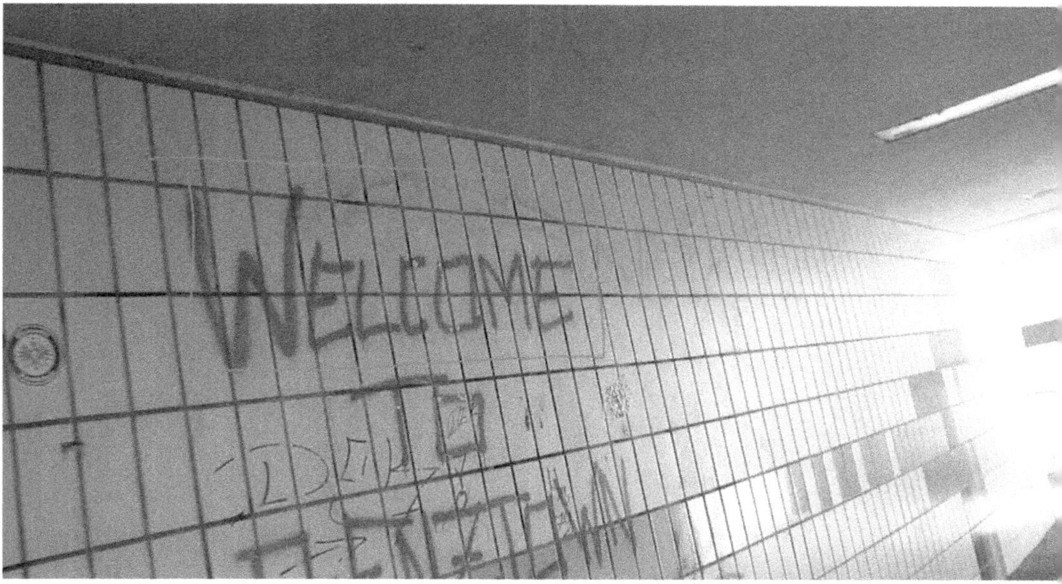

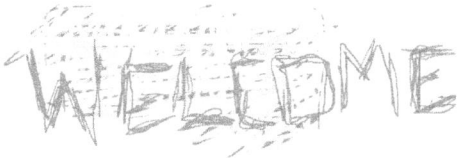

NOTES / NOTIZEN

Talking about showing work. My changing attitude to showing work. Slowly exhibiting publishing displaying making available. Being seen. Allowing others to see it. Inviting others to experience the work. Inviting others to experience the work. I still don't find it necessary.

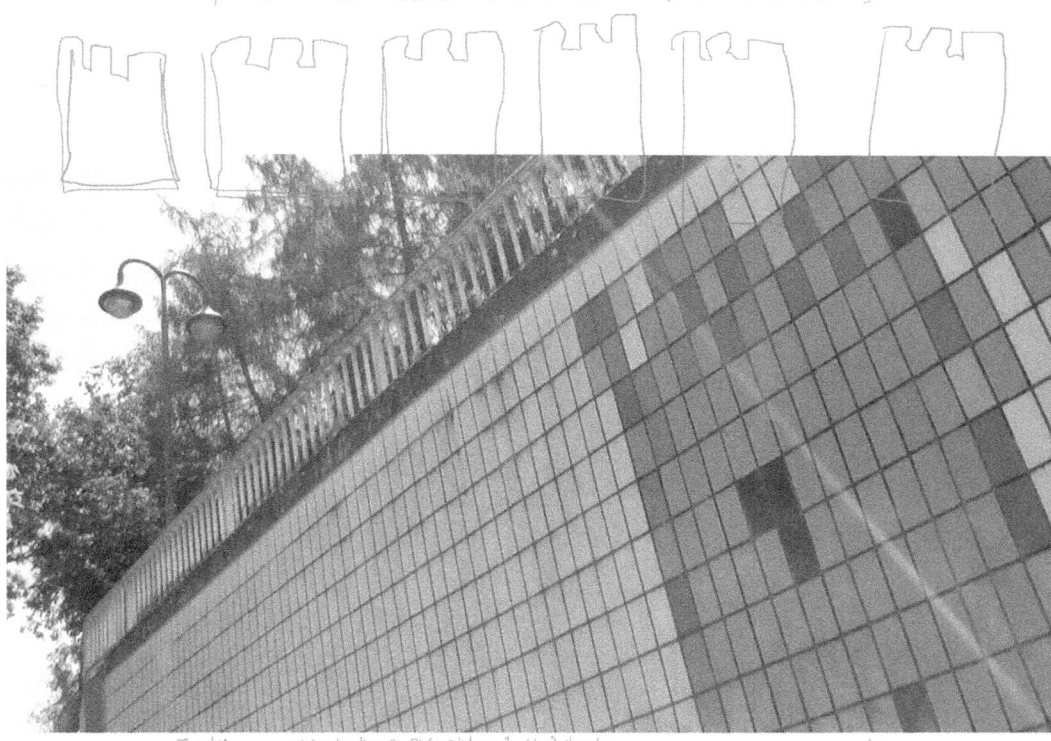

Twenty upper gate tower. prisoner's tower? Niederbrechen

The 20 metre high upper gate tower/prisoners tower in Niederbrechen is a tower remaining from the medieval city walls built town
1367 and 1379
between 1367 to 1379. There was also a gate but this was demolished in 1852. The town wall had six more towers and two
6 2

gates but they were wooden structures and have not survived. Replaced by an arch covered in ROSES.

This however in ceramic tiles in the shape of a tower in the subway that runs underneath the train tracks.

NOTES / NOTIZEN

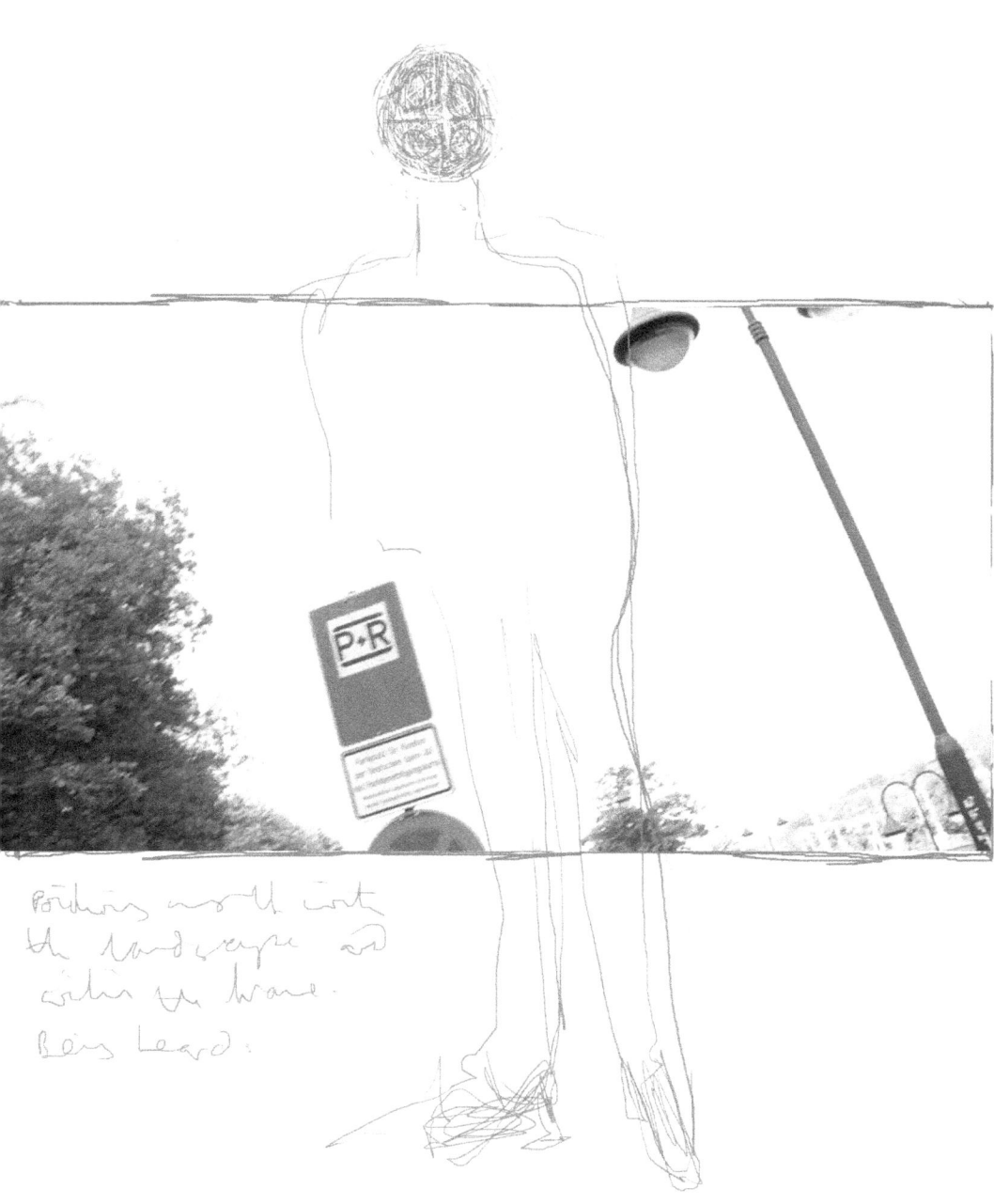

Polishing would with
the landscape and
within the frame.
Being heard.

NOTES / NOTIZEN

00:47:38 Here's the back of the station. There's a bush in the way.

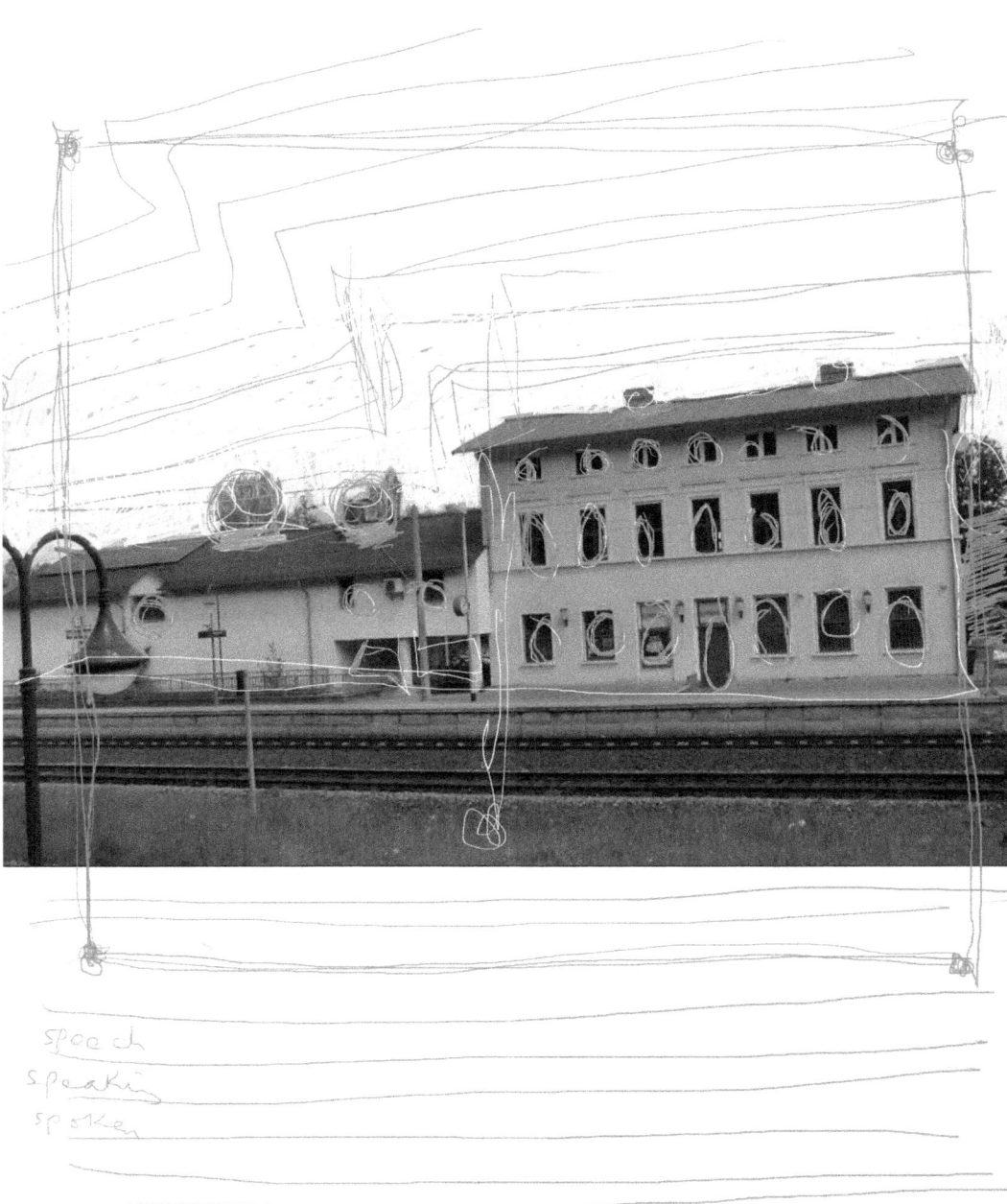

speech
speaking
spoken

NOTES / NOTIZEN

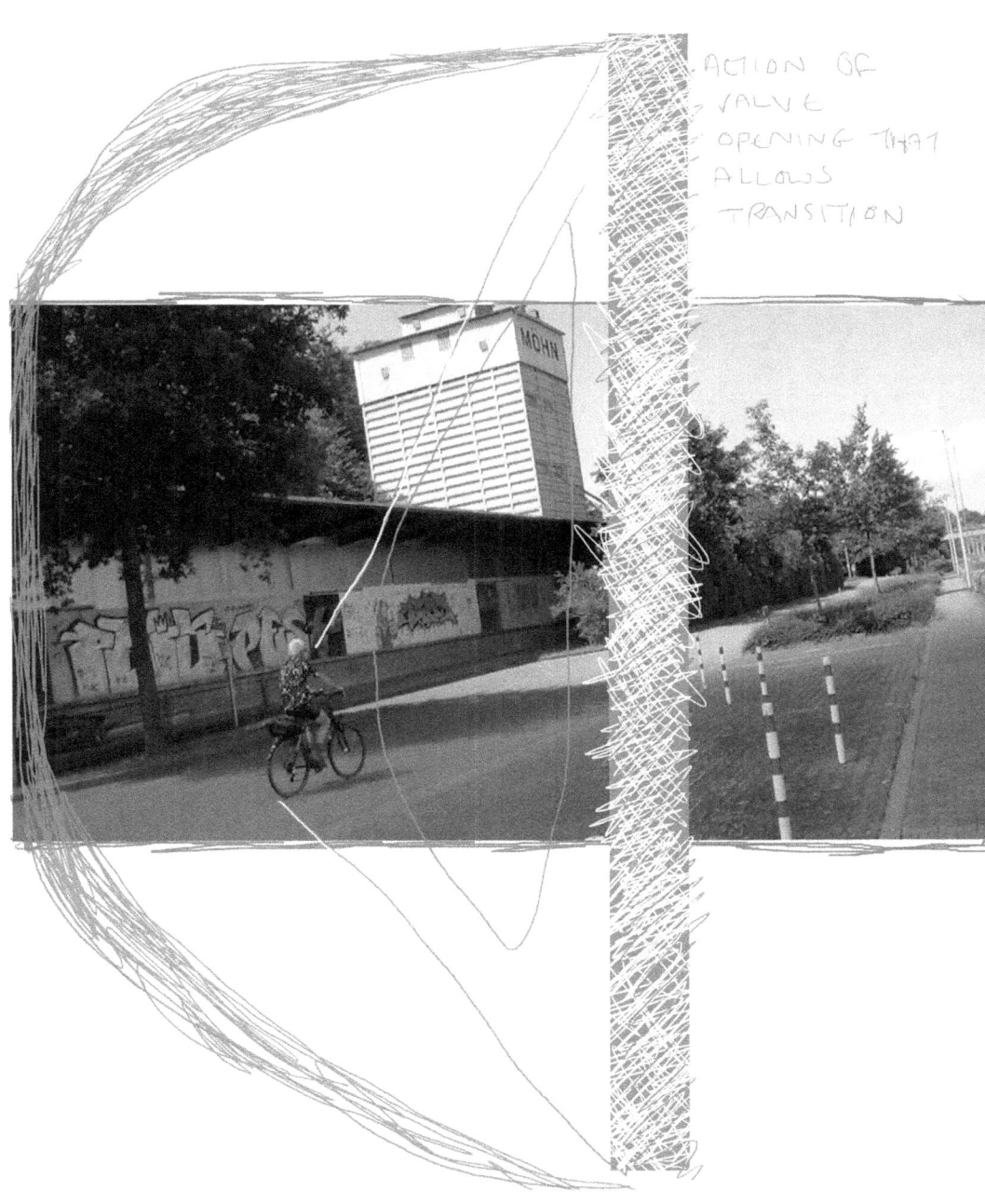

ACTION OF
VALVE
OPENING THAT
ALLOWS
TRANSITION

NOTES / NOTIZEN

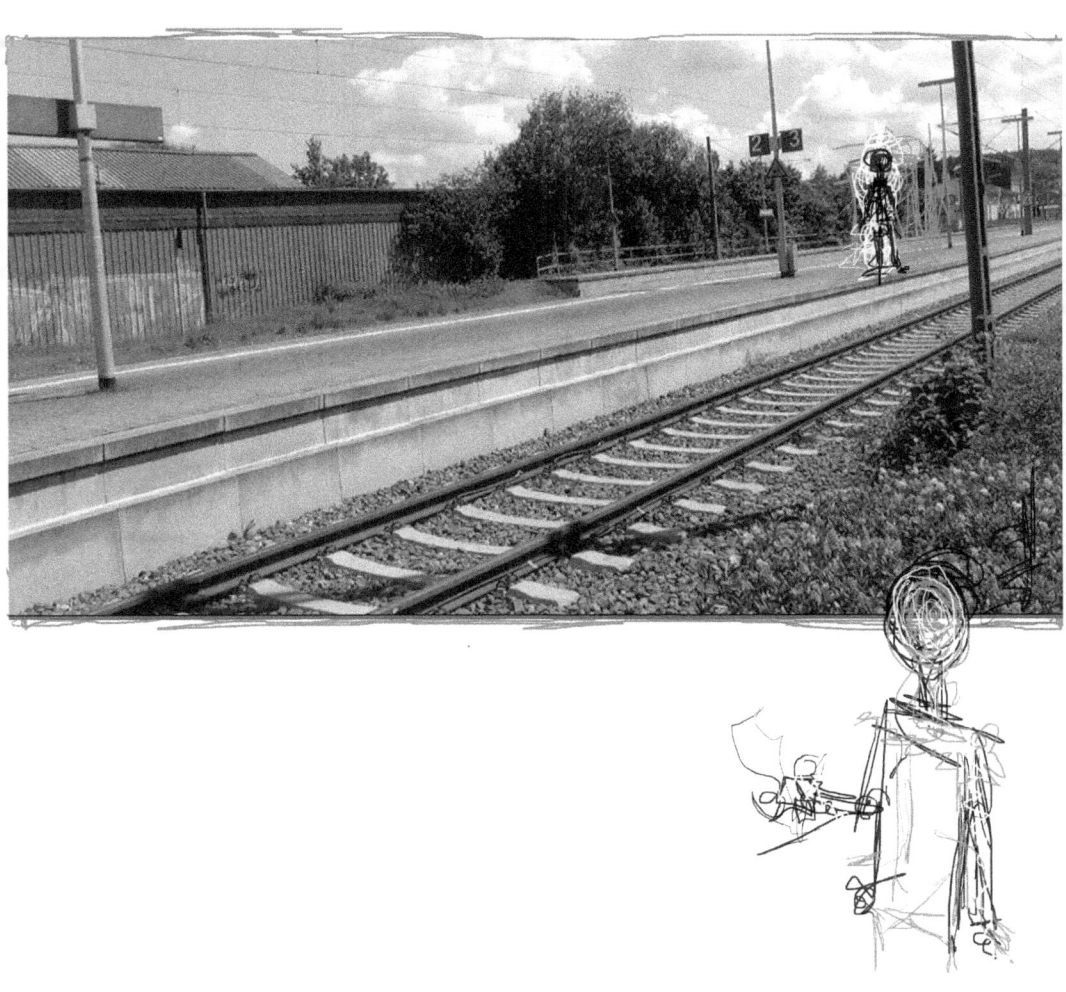

NOTES / NOTIZEN

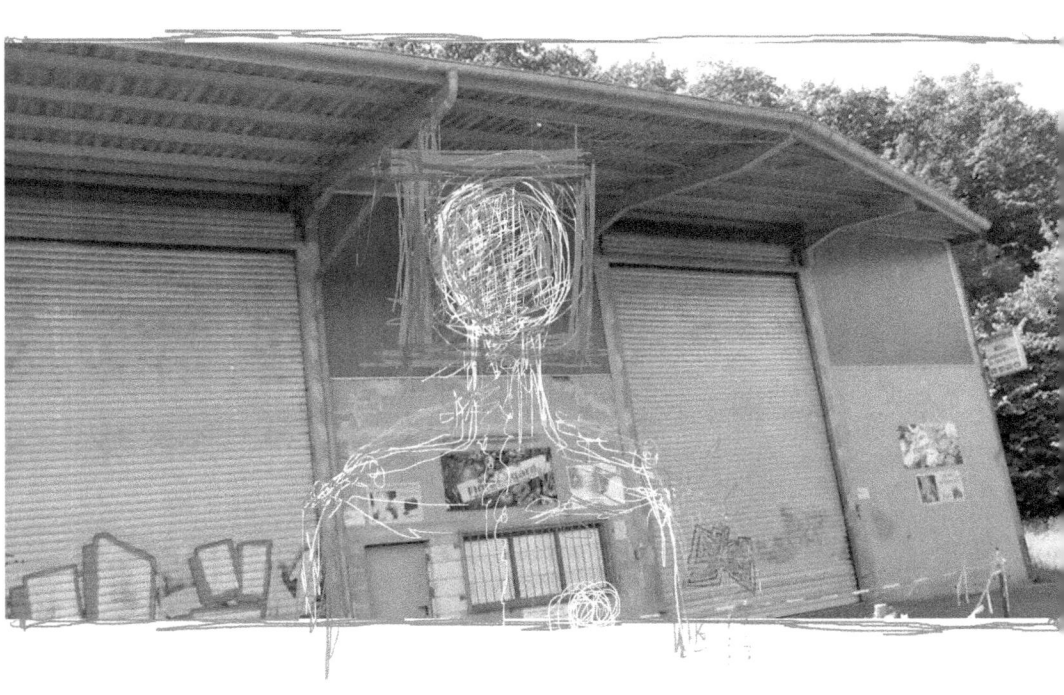

NOTES / NOTIZEN

00:54:19 I am walking.

00:54:27 And talking.

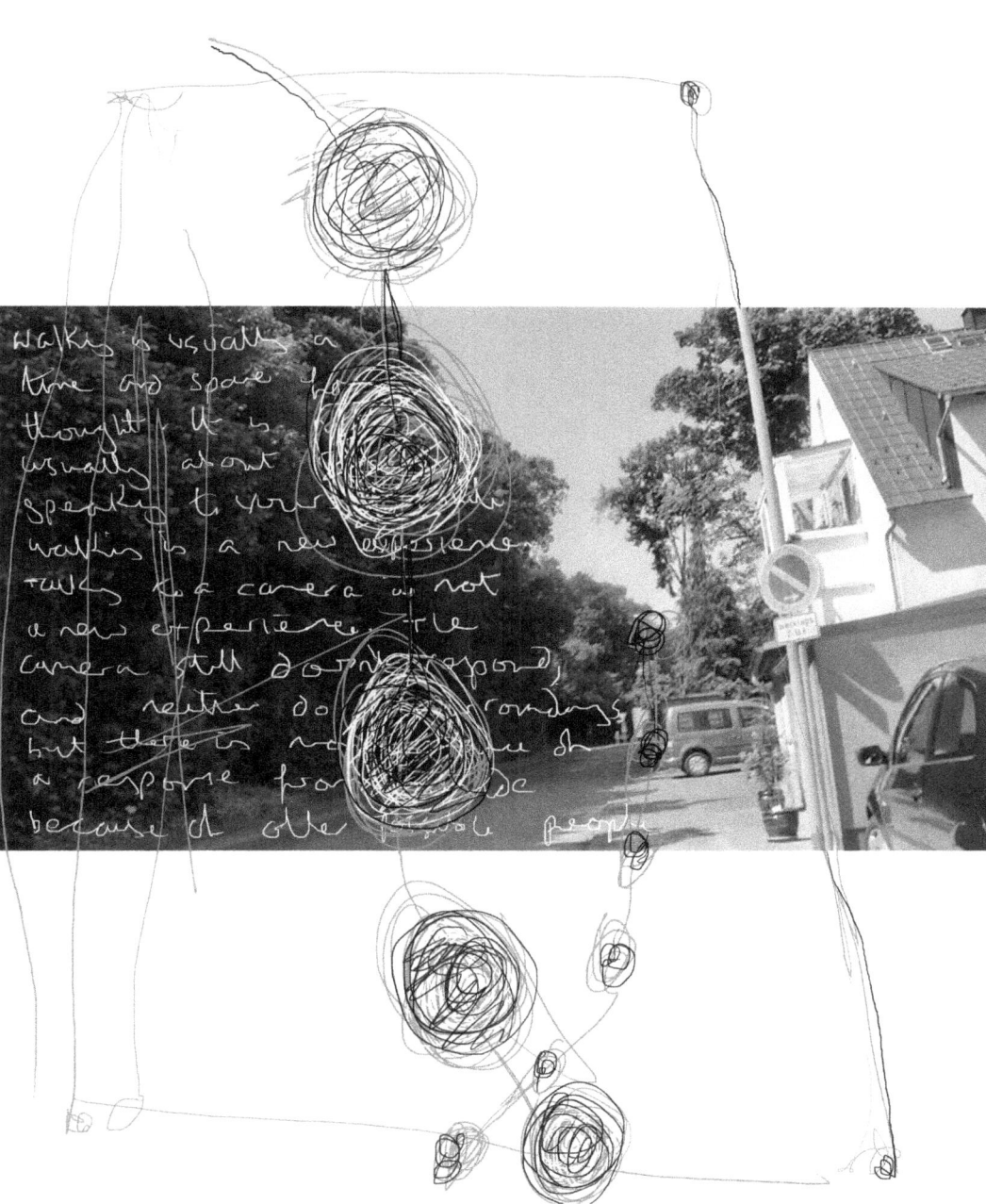

NOTES / NOTIZEN

00:55:23 There's the other side of the sign.

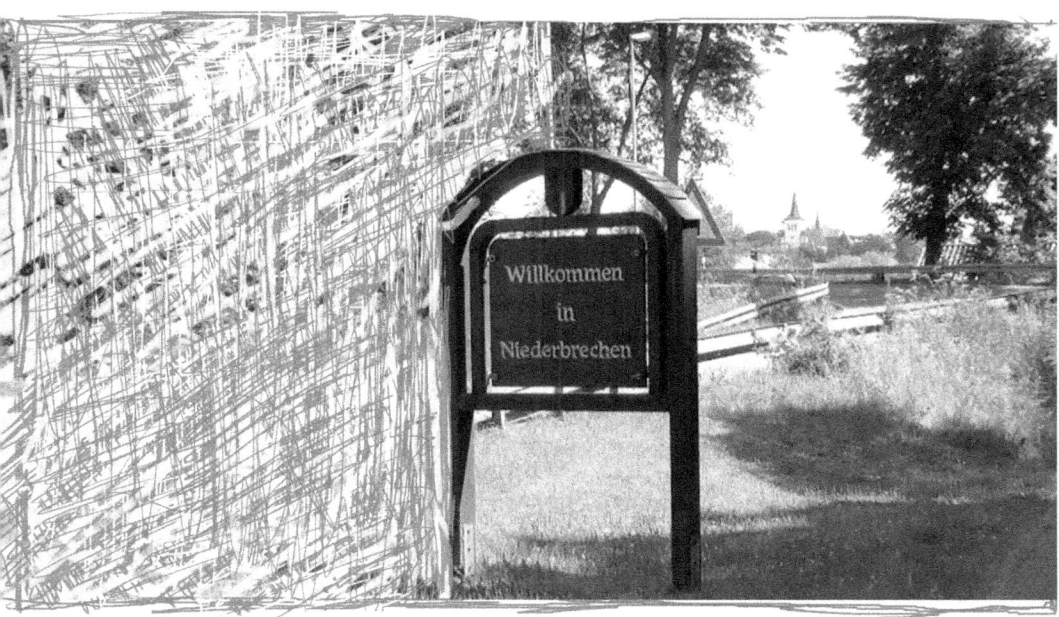

WILLKOMMEN

NOTES / NOTIZEN

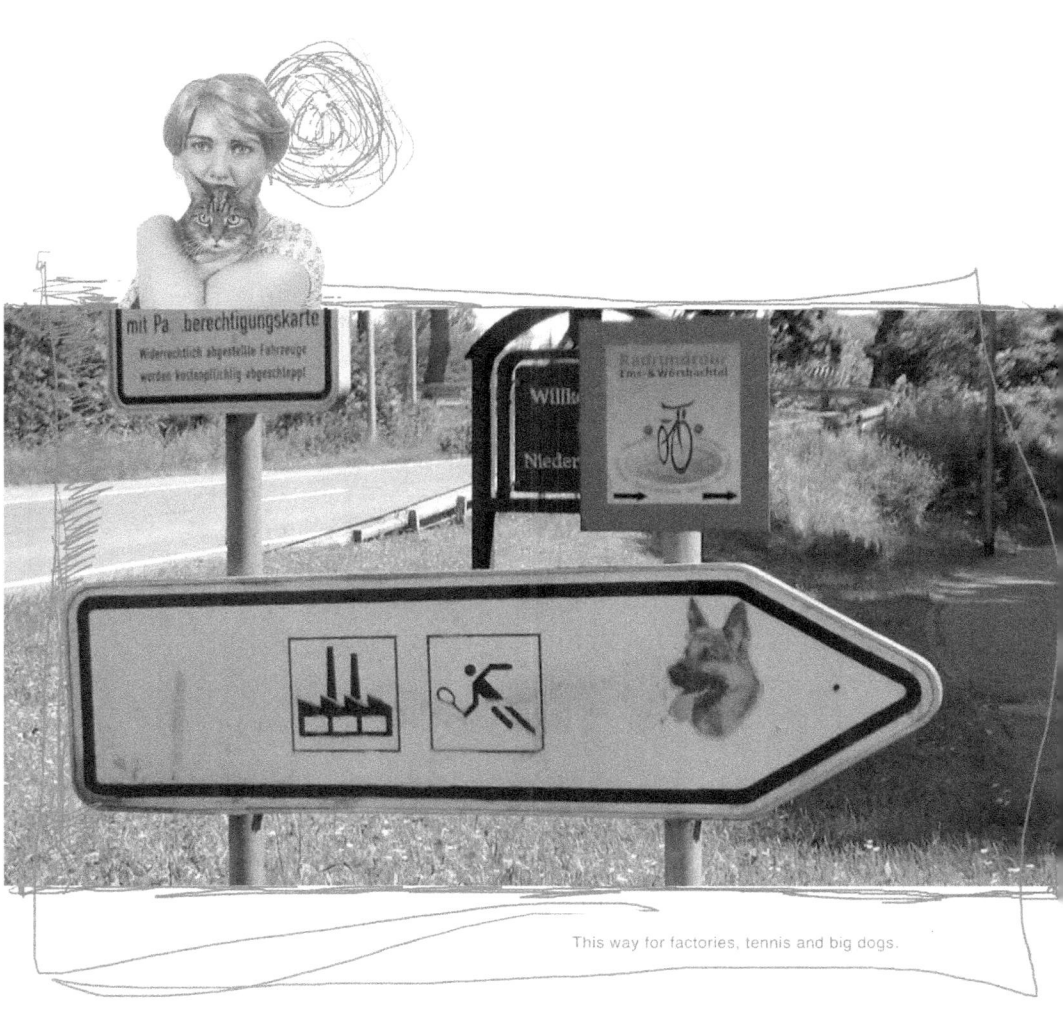

mit Pa berechtigungskarte

Widerrechtlich abgestellte Fahrzeuge
werden kostenpflichtig abgeschleppt

Willk

Nieder

This way for factories, tennis and big dogs.

NOTES / NOTIZEN

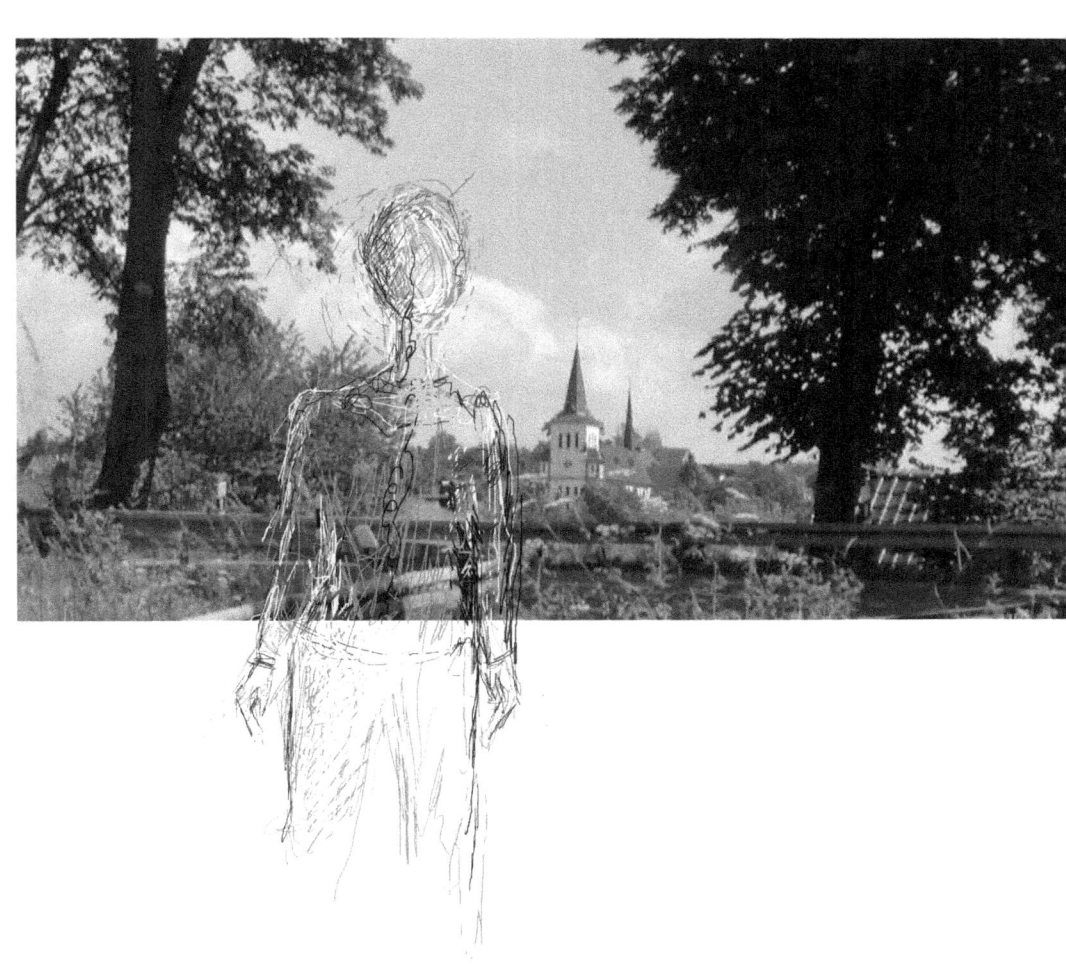

NOTES / NOTIZEN

This house looks a bit like my house

little train

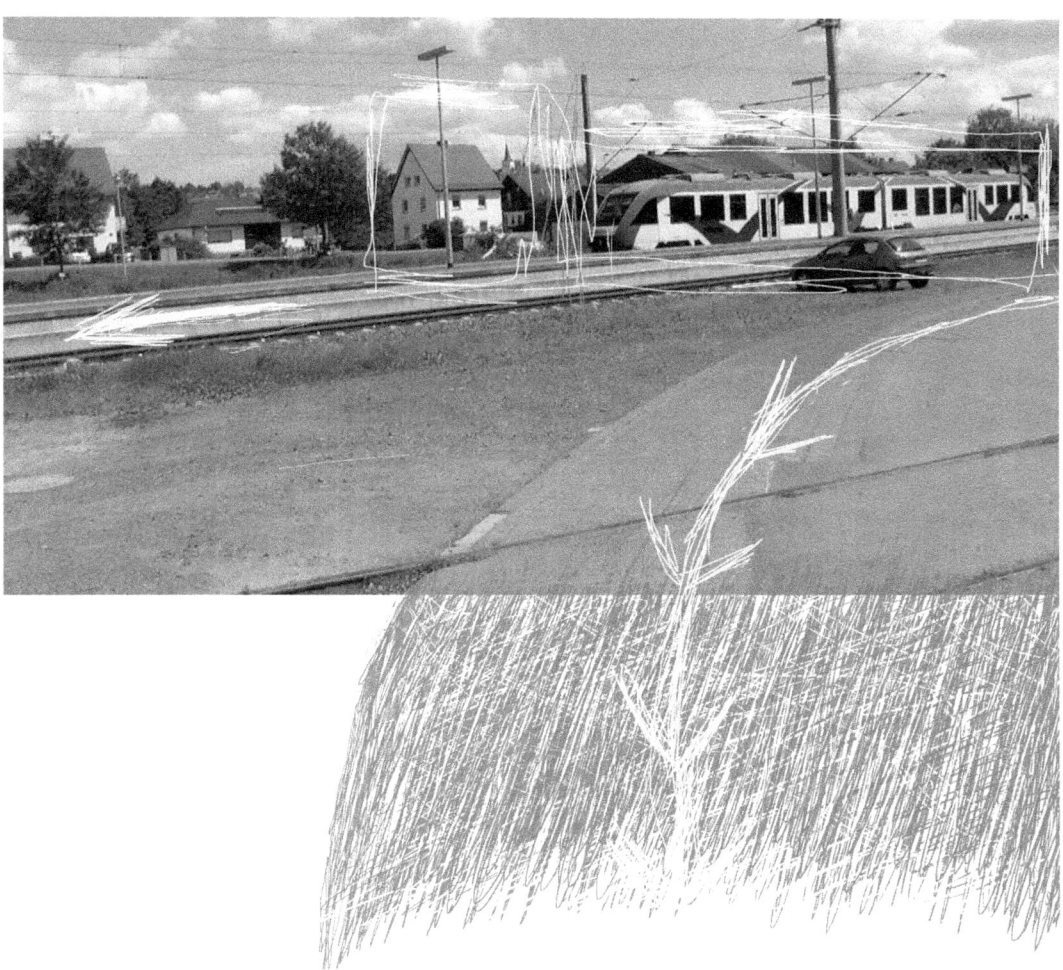

NOTES / NOTIZEN

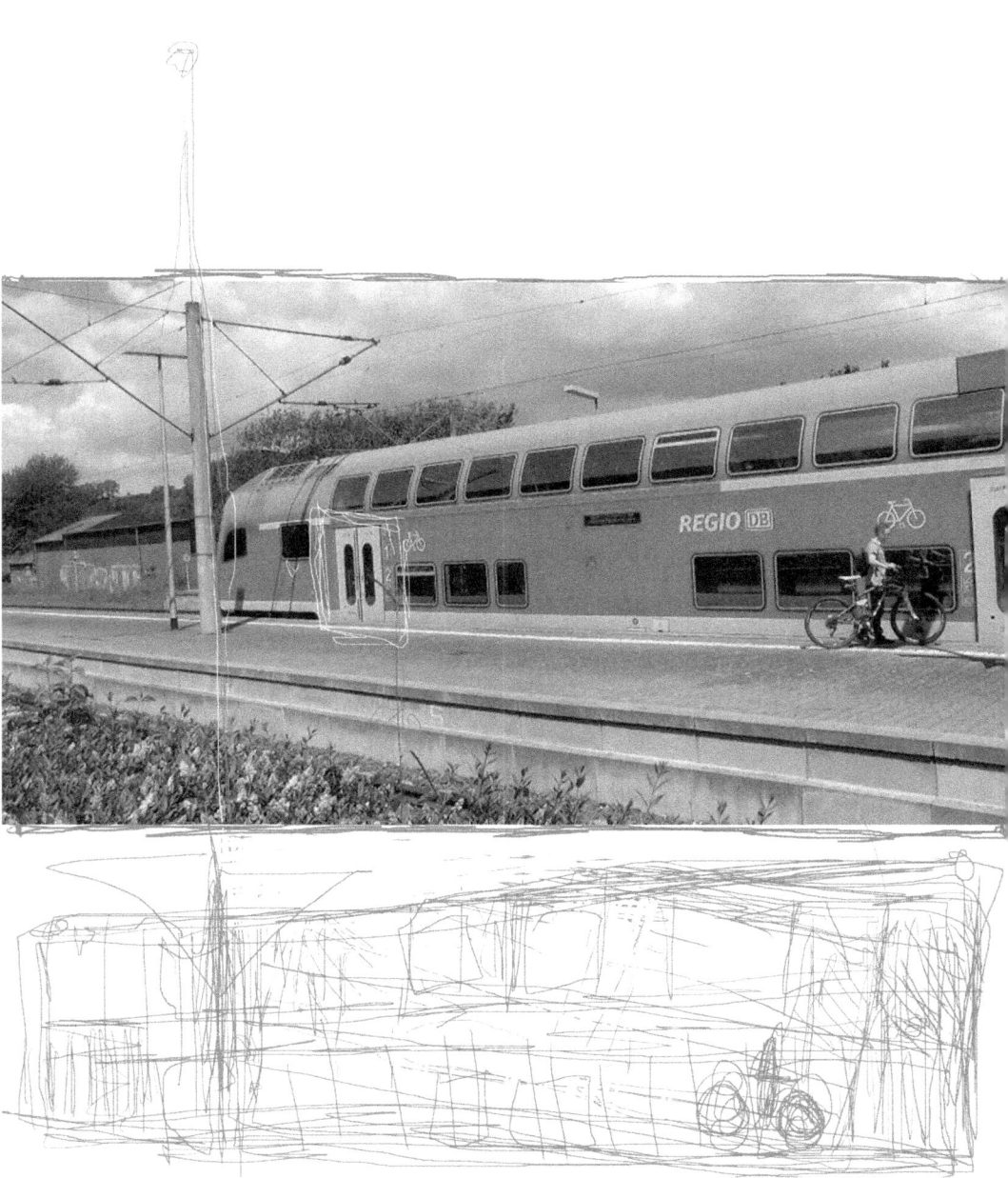

NOTES / NOTIZEN

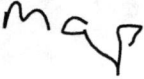

I love this place so much.
I love this place so much.
I love this place so much
Say it out loud to the place. Tell the
place that you love it.
'I love this place so much.'

VALVE

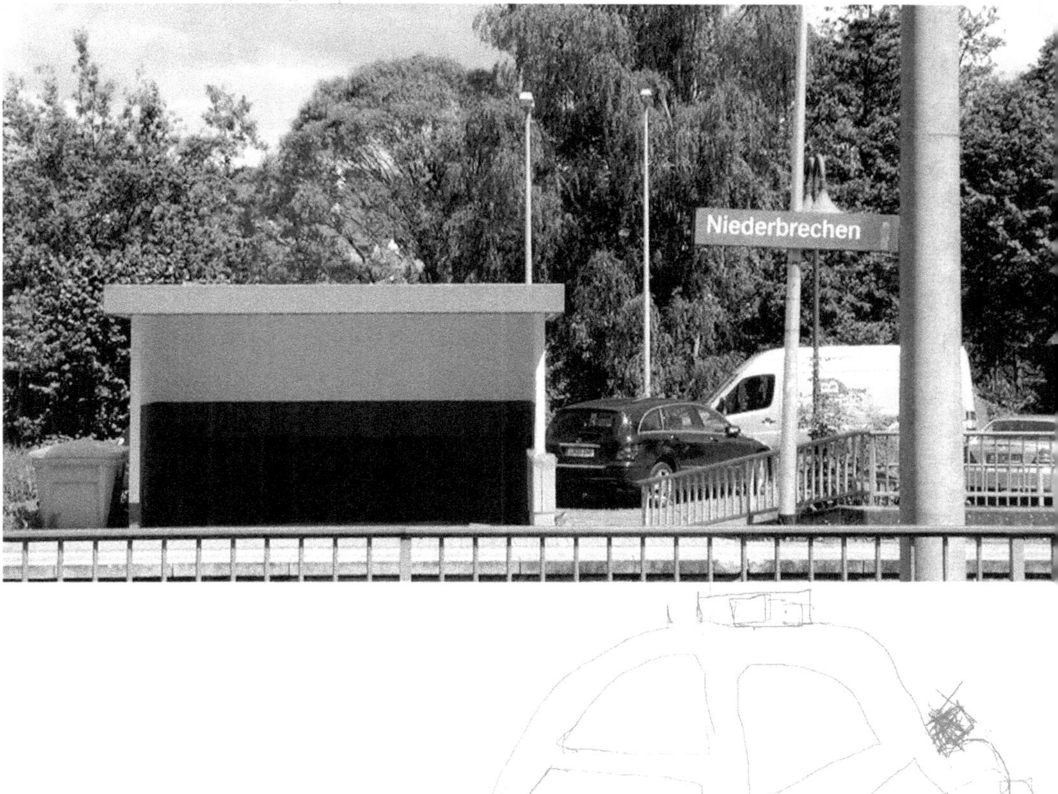

Niederbrechen

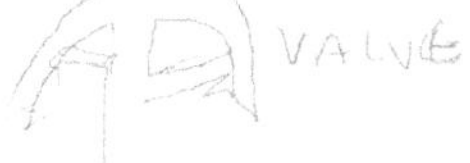

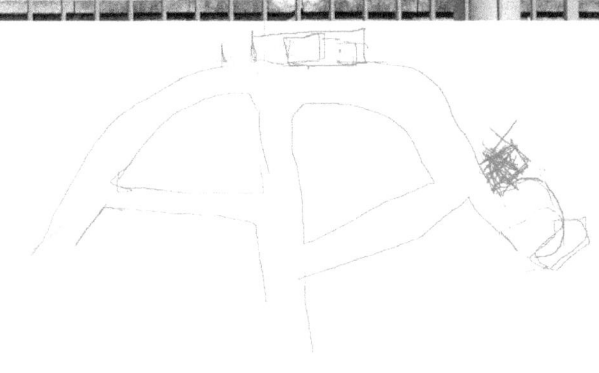

NOTES / NOTIZEN

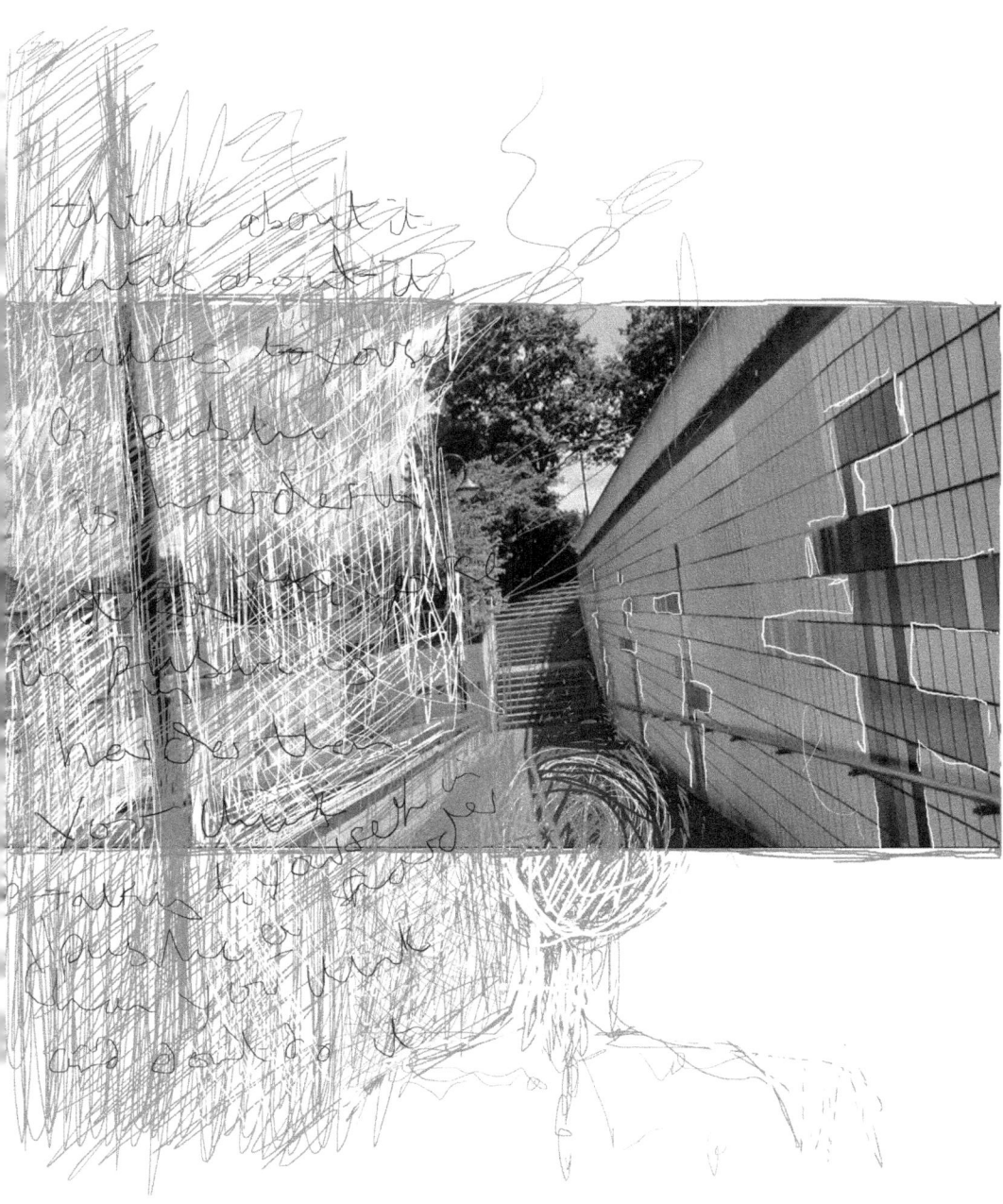

NOTES / NOTIZEN

heute

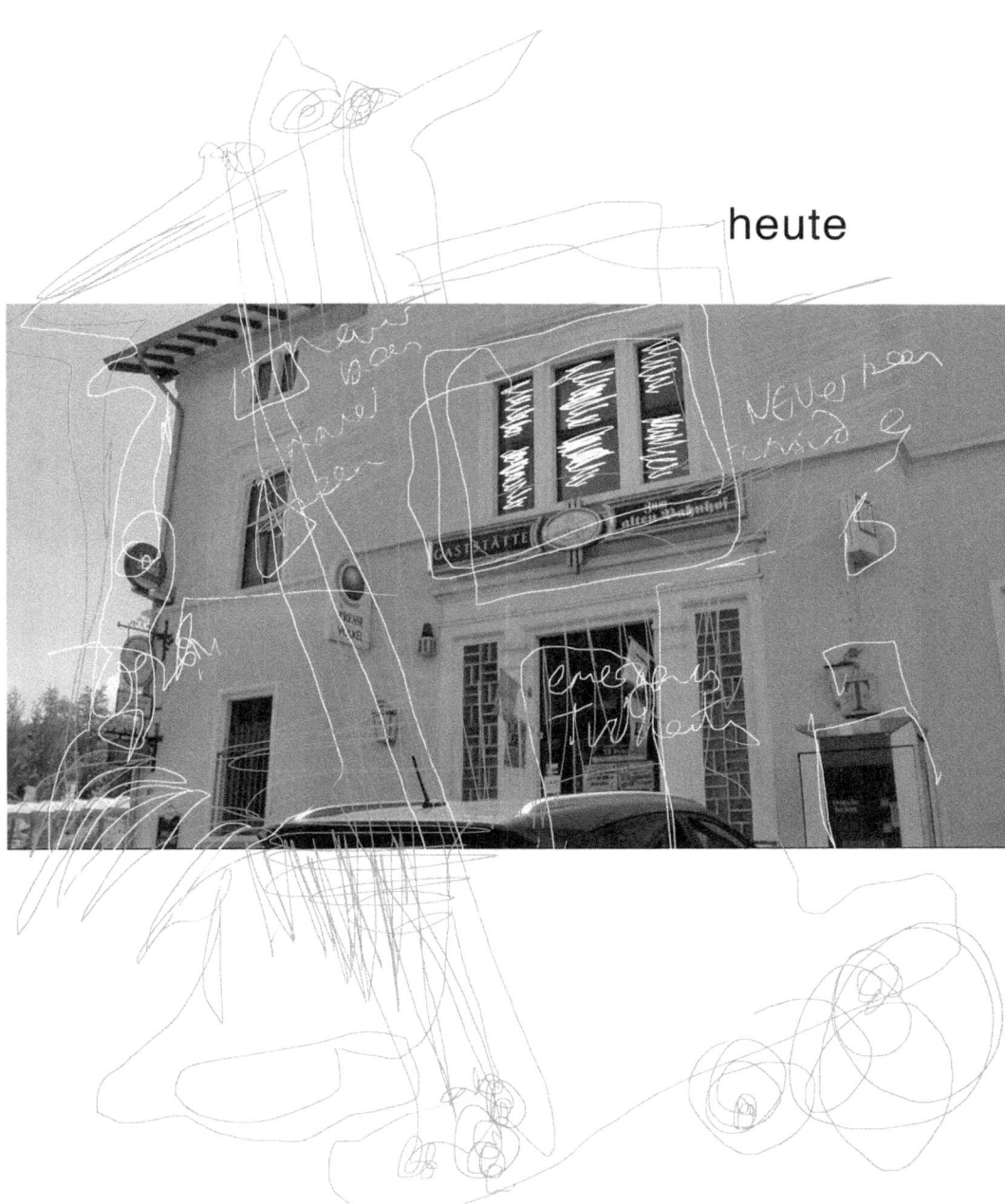

NOTES / NOTIZEN

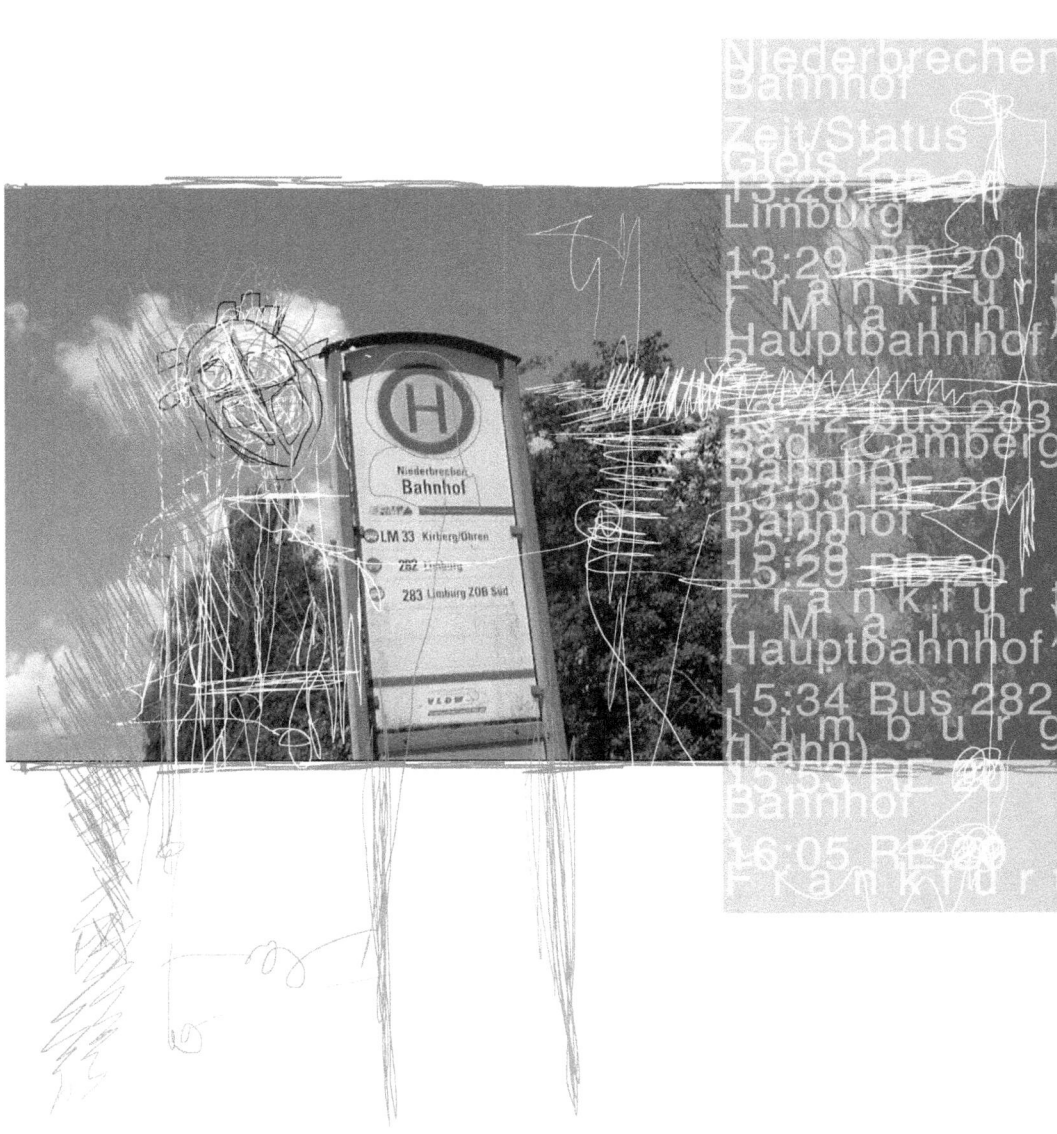

NOTES / NOTIZEN

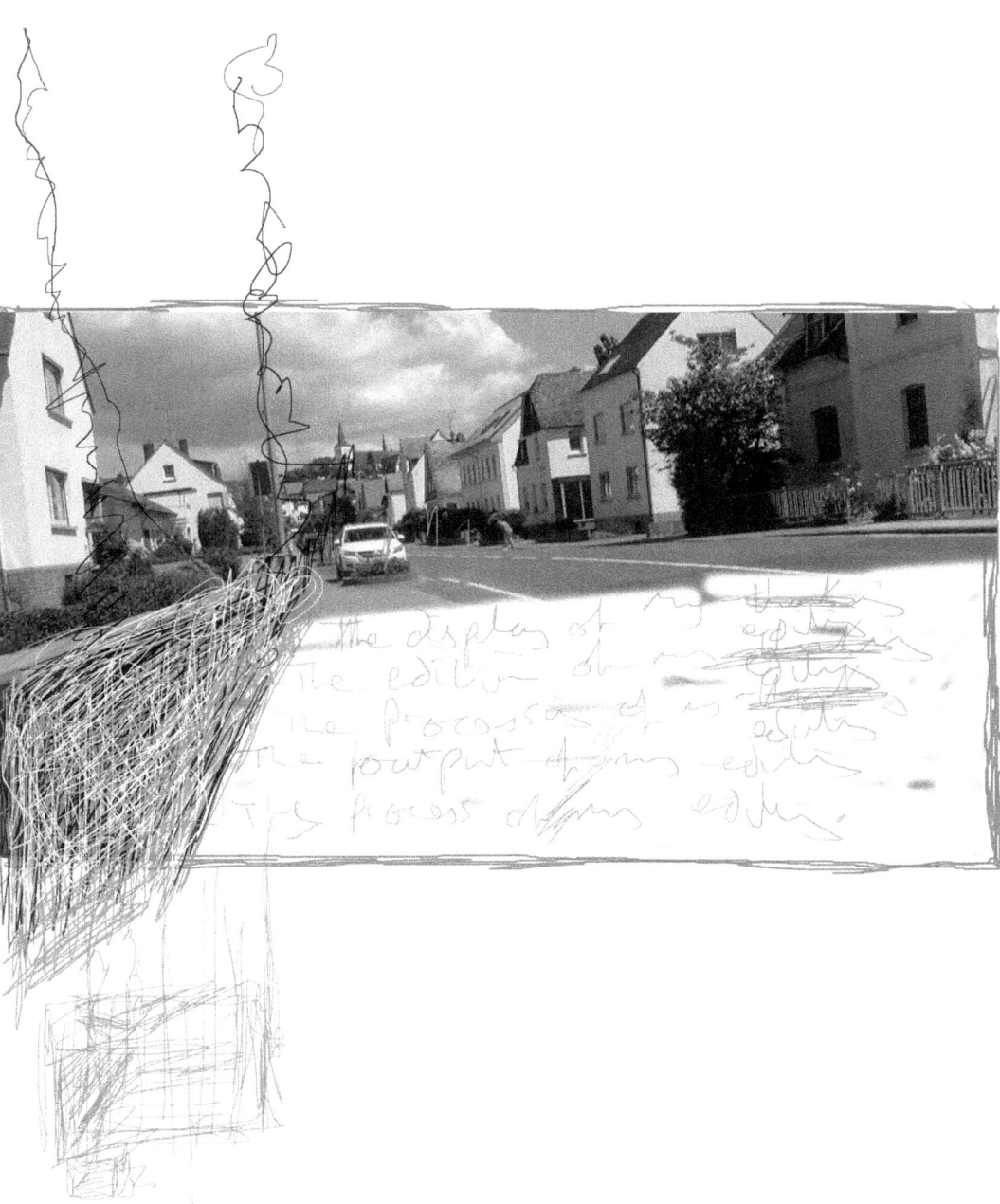

NOTES / NOTIZEN

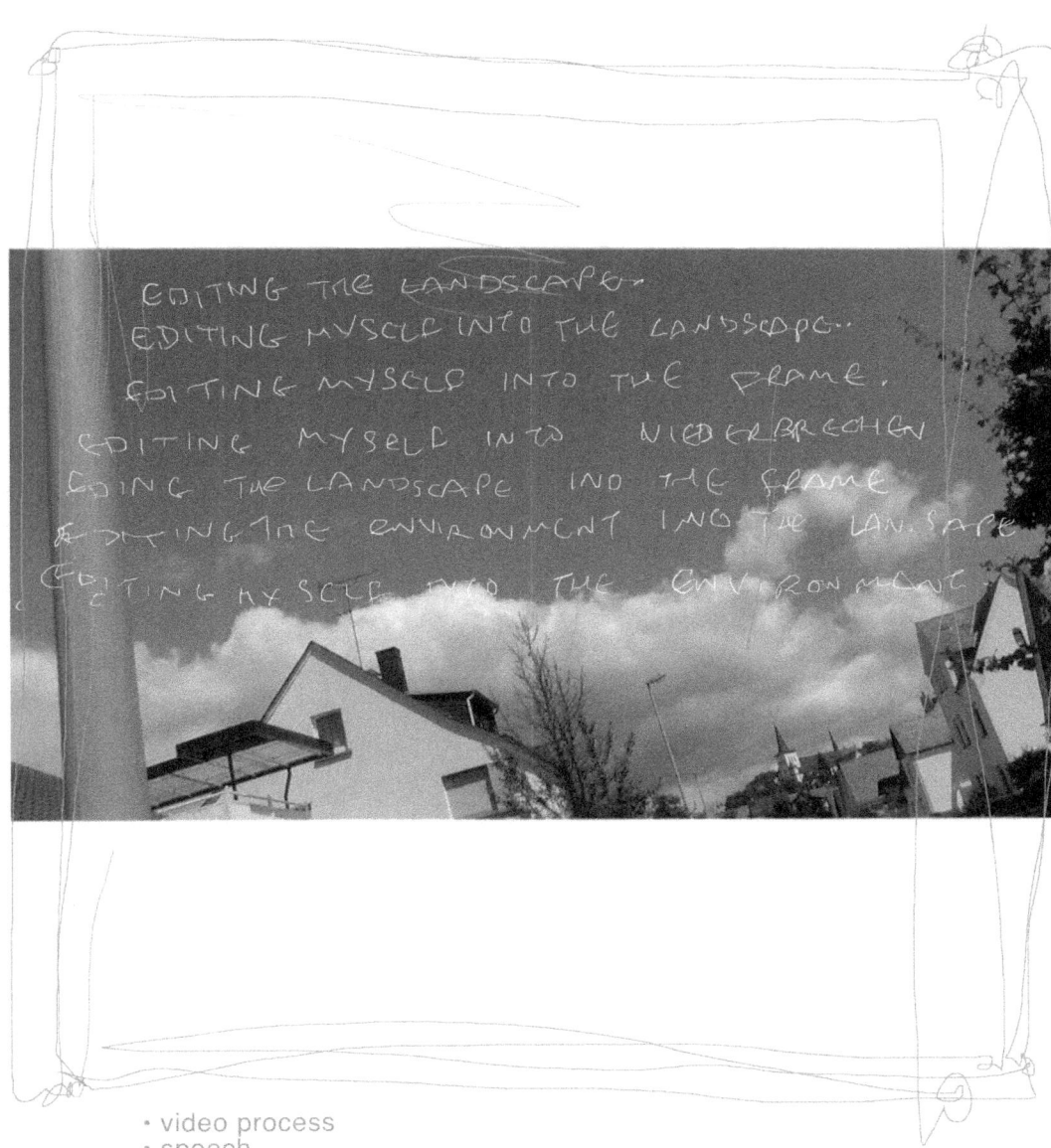

- video process
- speech
- drawing & text

NOTES / NOTIZEN

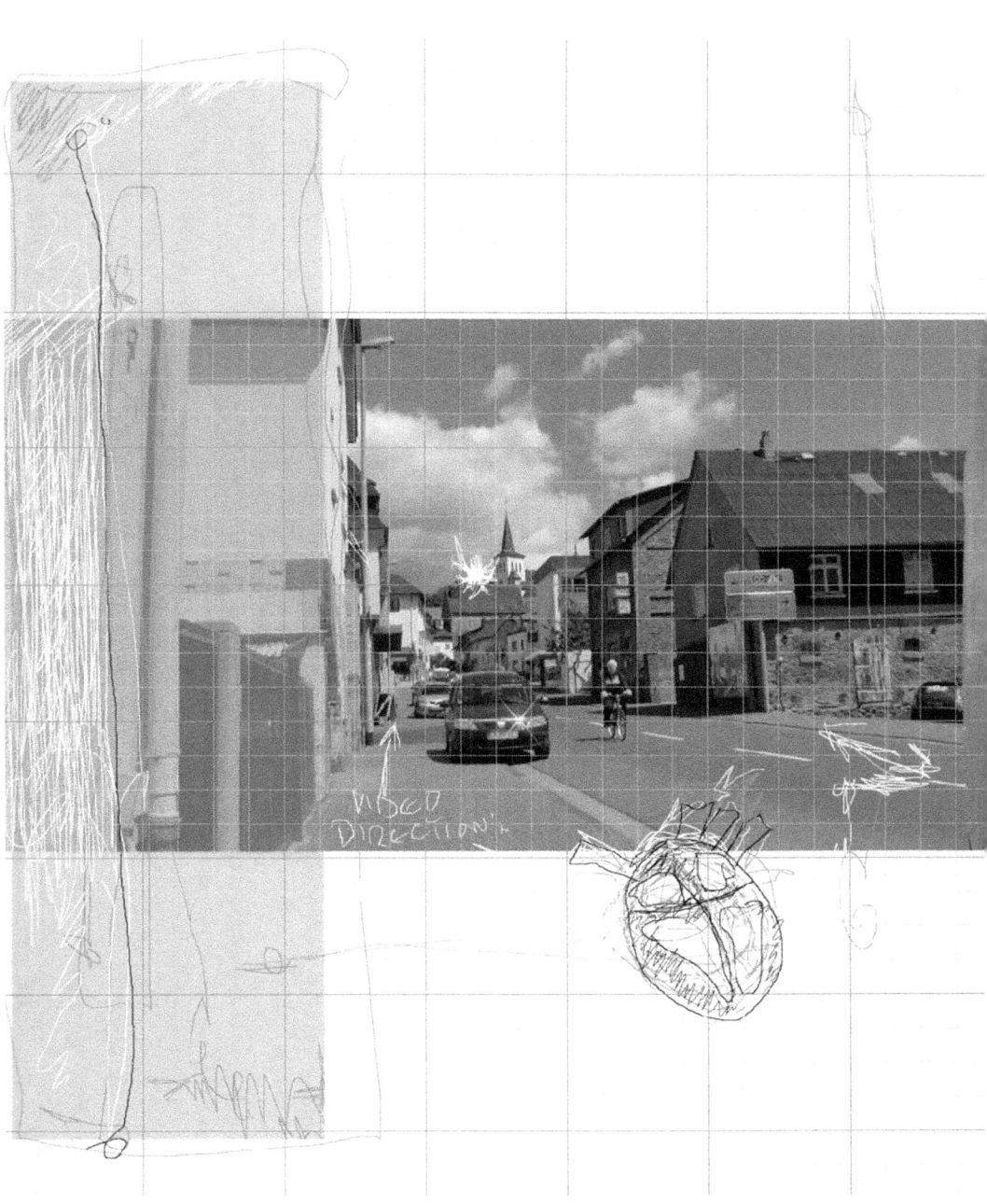

NOTES / NOTIZEN

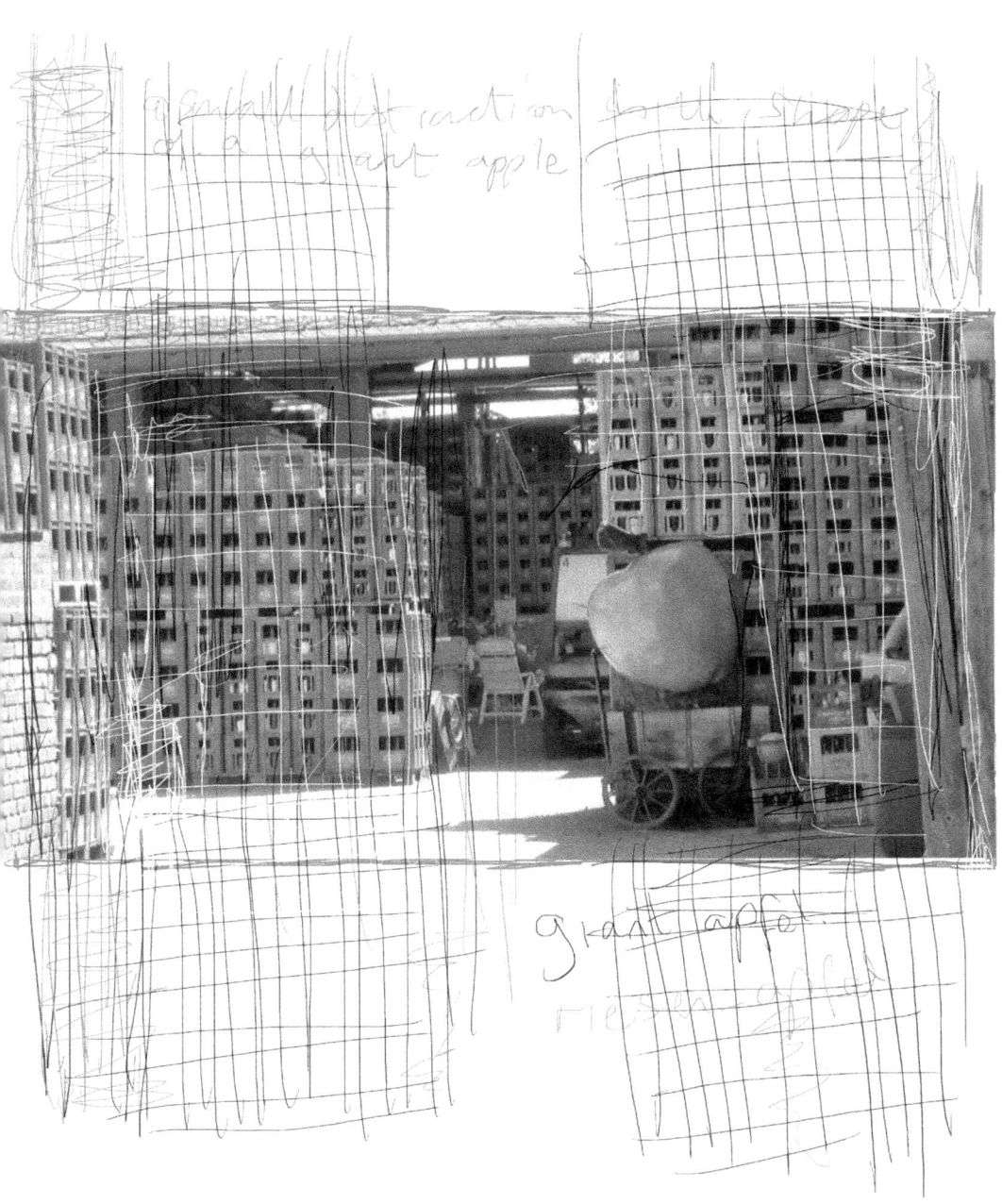

NOTES / NOTIZEN

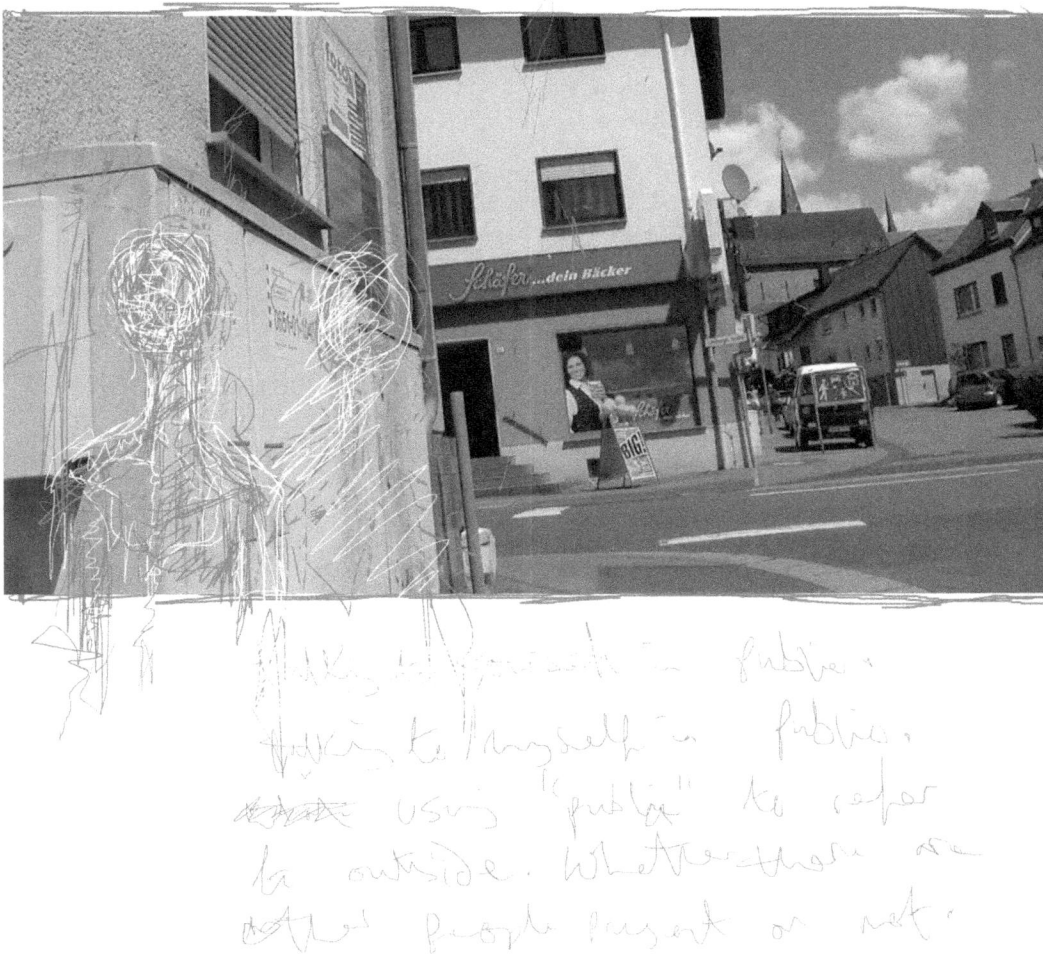

Making yourself in public.
talking to yourself in public.
~~using~~ using "public" to refer
to outside. Whether there are
~~other~~ people present or not.

NOTES / NOTIZEN

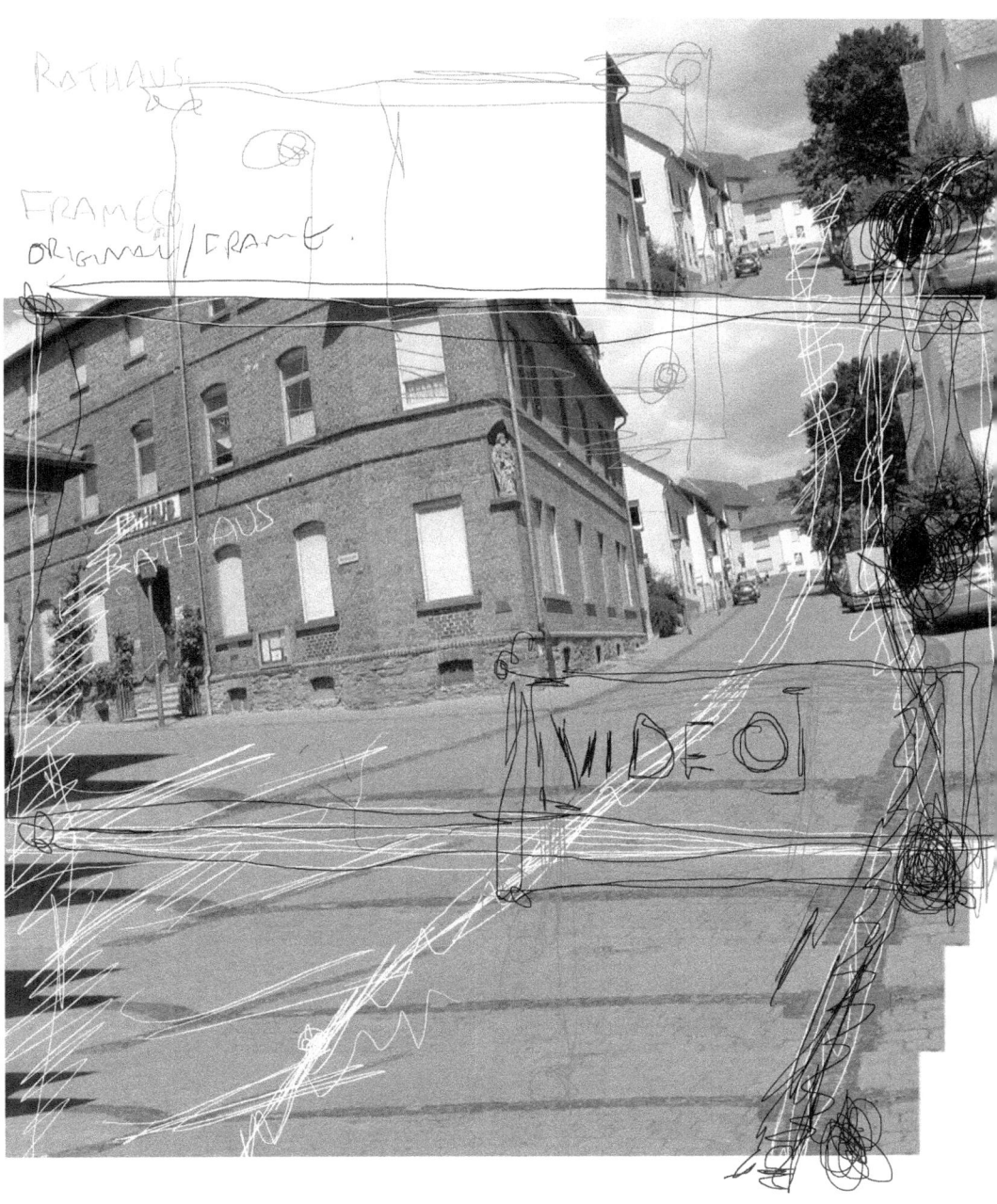

NOTES / NOTIZEN

FOUNTAIN / NIEDERBRECHEN

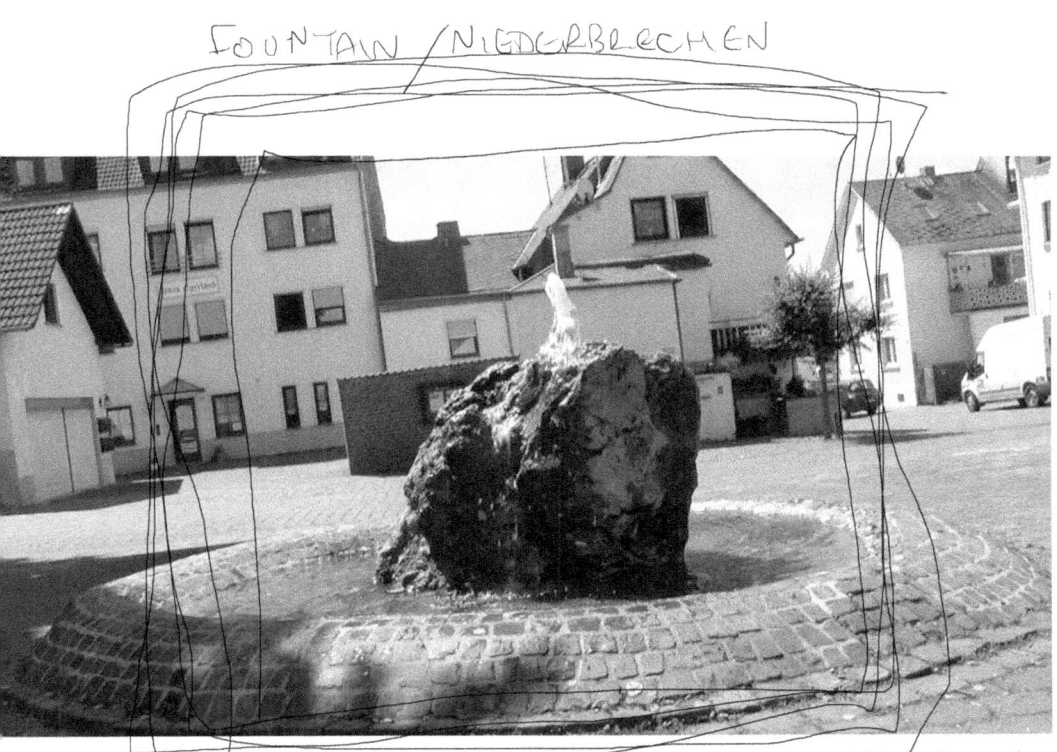

There is much to be said about this fountain. I didn't know it was a fountain bcause the water was turned off in the winter months. For a long time it was just an ugly chunk of rock with a dry moat arount it that announced that it was special in some way but there was no indication as to why it was special. Once the water was switched on and it became a fountain it made a little more sense but it was still just a large chunk of rock. As a fountain it remains pretty ugly, this image taken from the video actually makes it look nicer than it does in real life. There are many very beautiful fountains in Germany, such as the one on Königsallee in Düsseldorf, but the fountain in Niederbrechen is not one of them.

There are many very beautiful things in Niederbrechen (but this isn't one of them).

NOTES / NOTIZEN

I have a lot to say about the environment, and my emotional response to the environment, and less to say about the process.

This is the most beautiful place.
I love it here.

NOTES / NOTIZEN

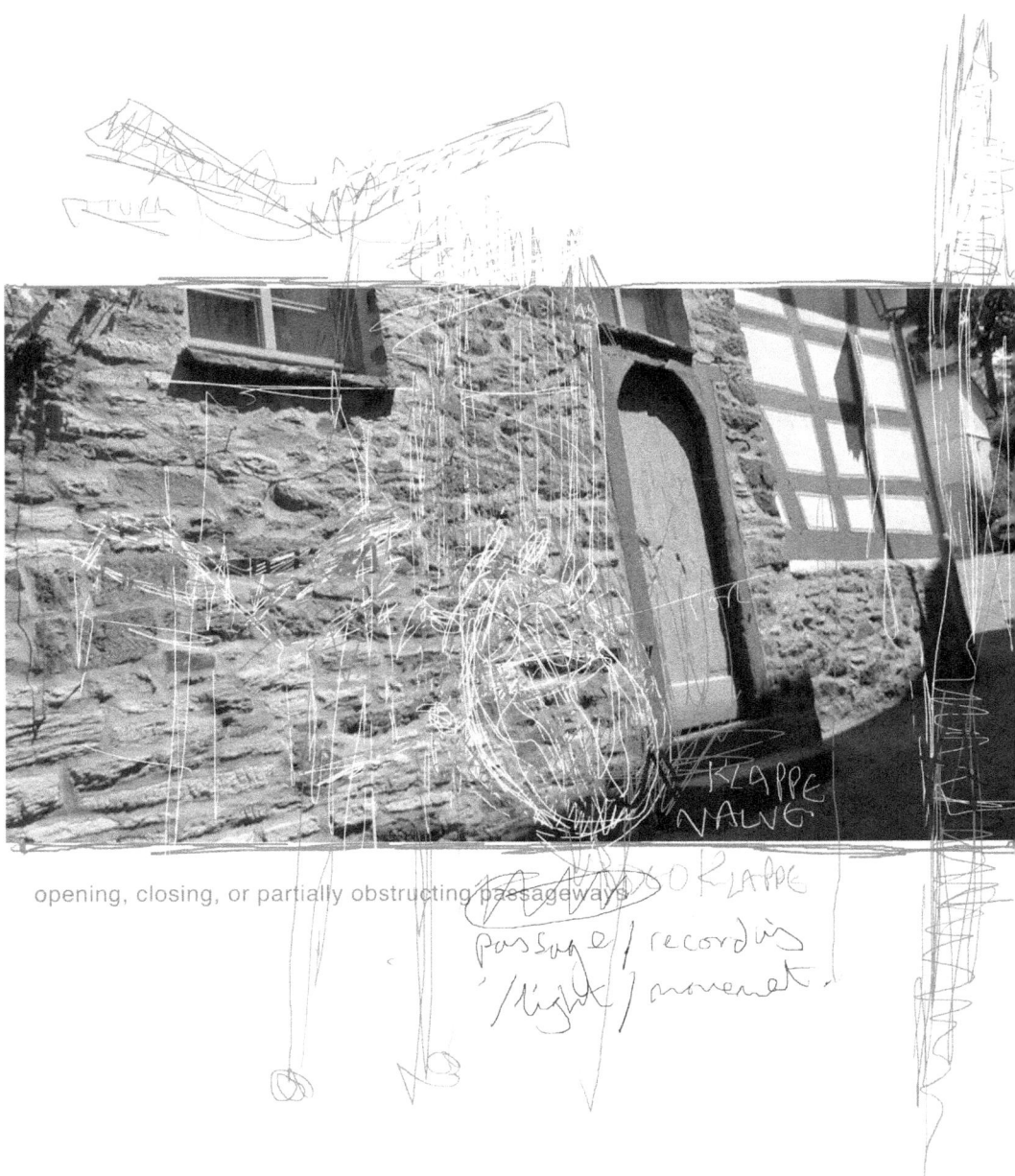

opening, closing, or partially obstructing passageways

NOTES / NOTIZEN

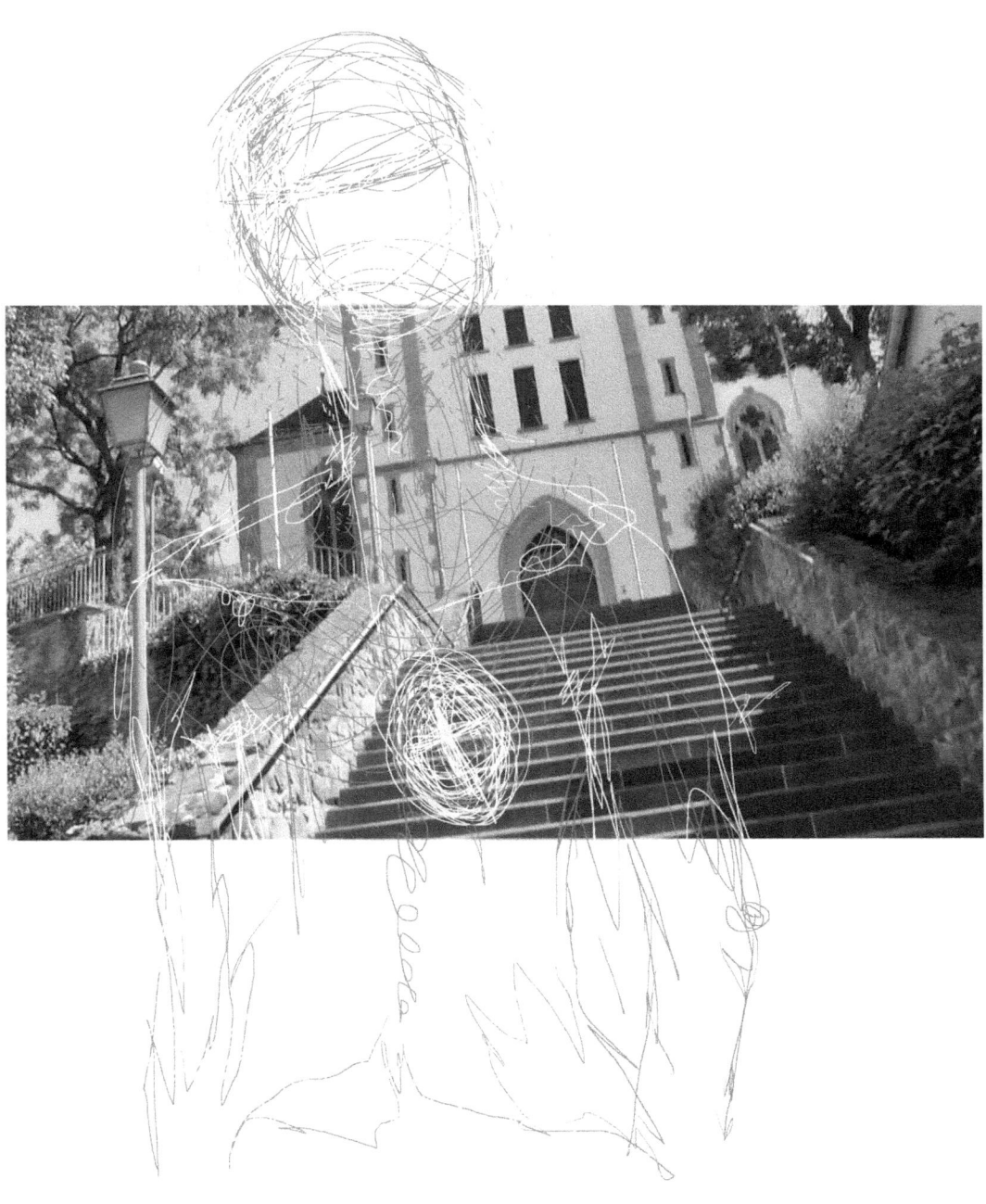

NOTES / NOTIZEN

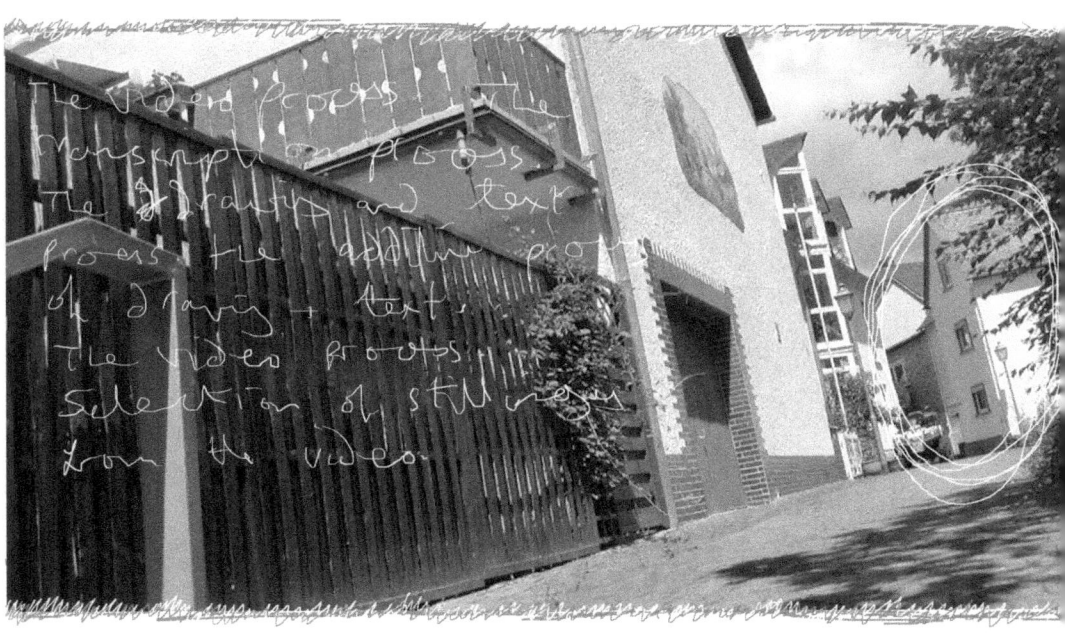

The video process. The
transcription process.
The of drawing and text
process. the adding process
of drawing + text.
The video process.
Selection of still images
from the video.

NOTES / NOTIZEN

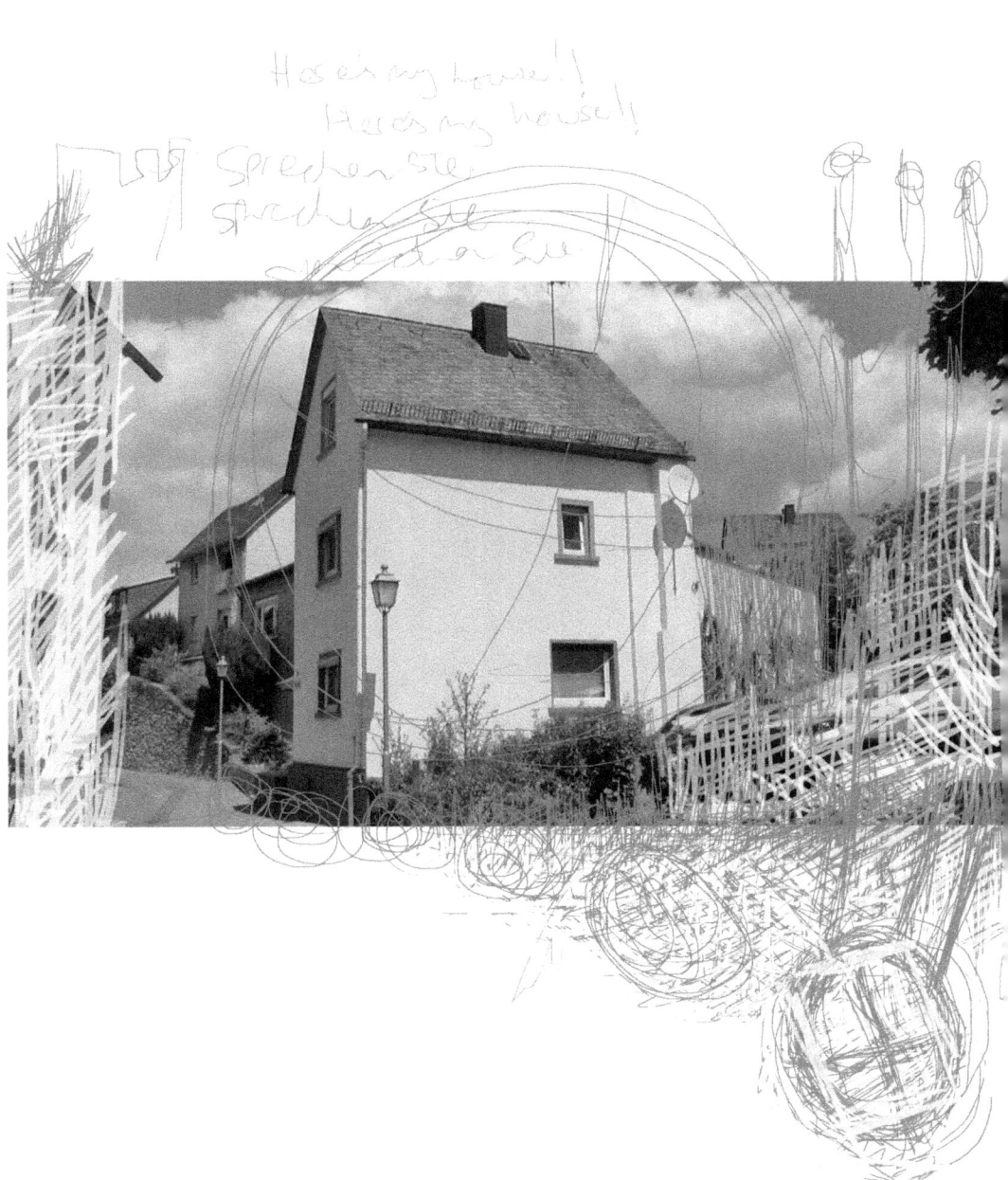

NOTES / NOTIZEN

TALKING WITH MY HANDS.
TALKING WITH MY HANDS
TALKING WITH MY HANDS

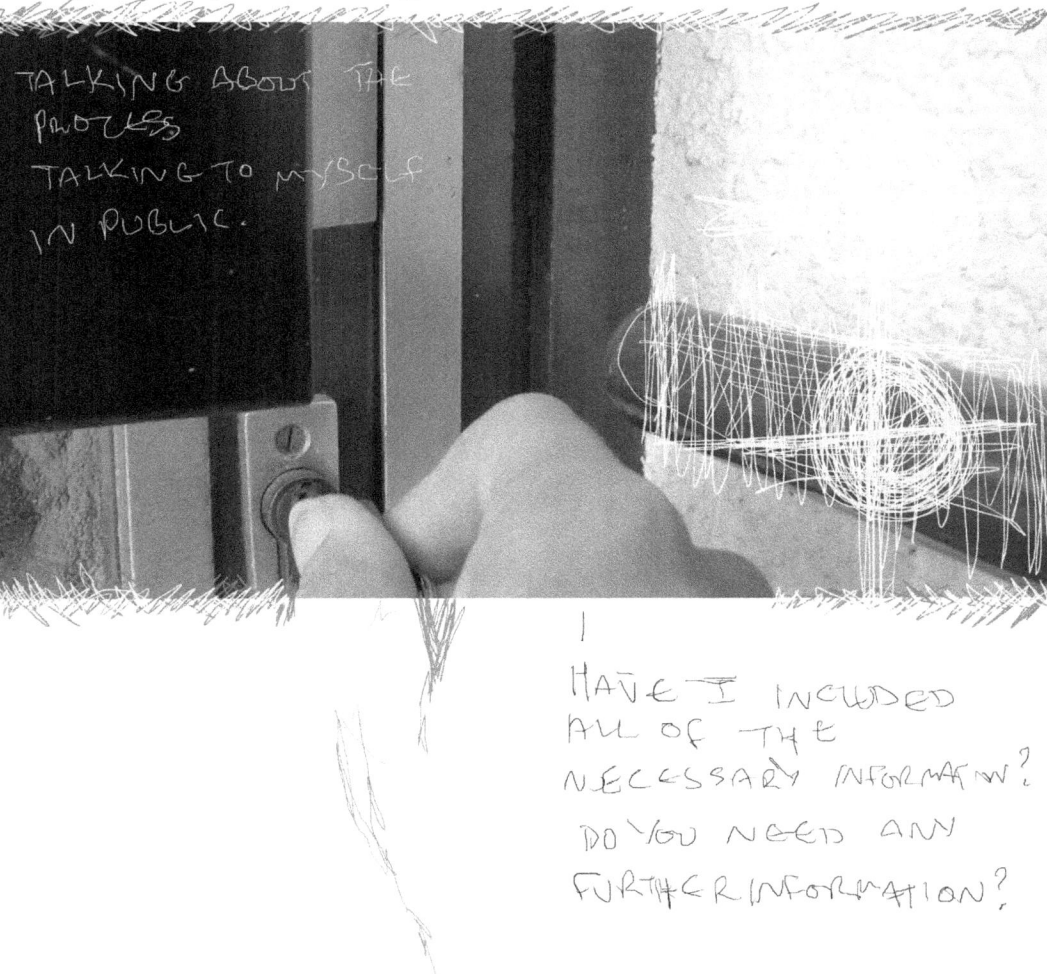

TALKING ABOUT THE
PROCESS
TALKING TO MYSELF
IN PUBLIC.

HAVE I INCLUDED
ALL OF THE
NECESSARY INFORMATION?
DO YOU NEED ANY
FURTHER INFORMATION?

NOTES / NOTIZEN

map

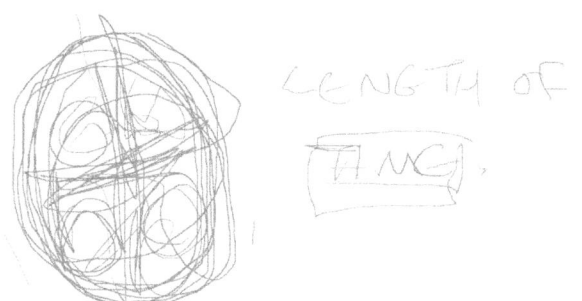

LENGTH OF.
[THING].

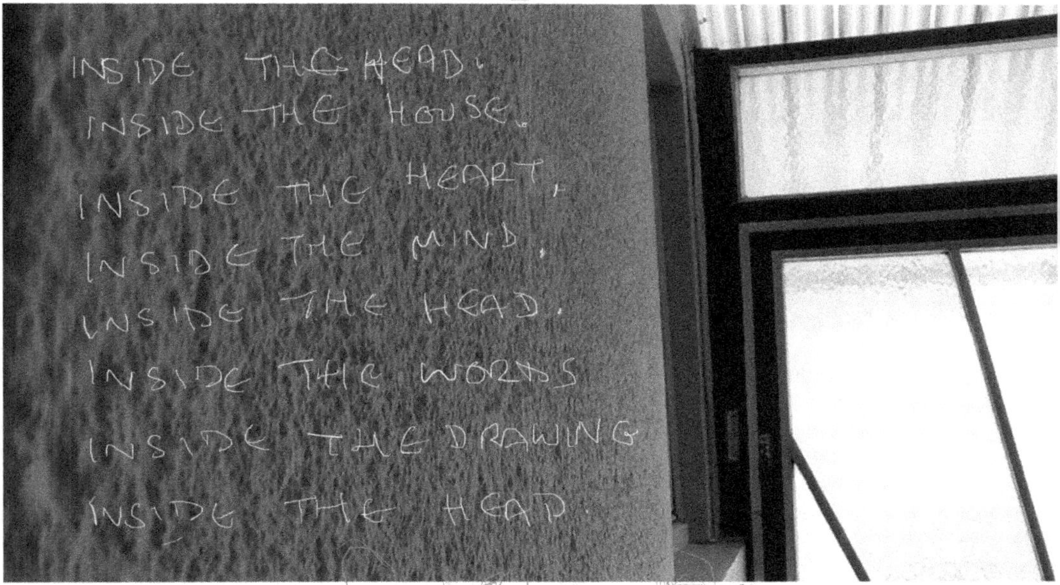

INSIDE THE HEAD.
INSIDE THE HOUSE.
INSIDE THE HEART,
INSIDE THE MIND,
INSIDE THE HEAD.
INSIDE THE WORDS
INSIDE THE DRAWING
INSIDE THE HEAD.

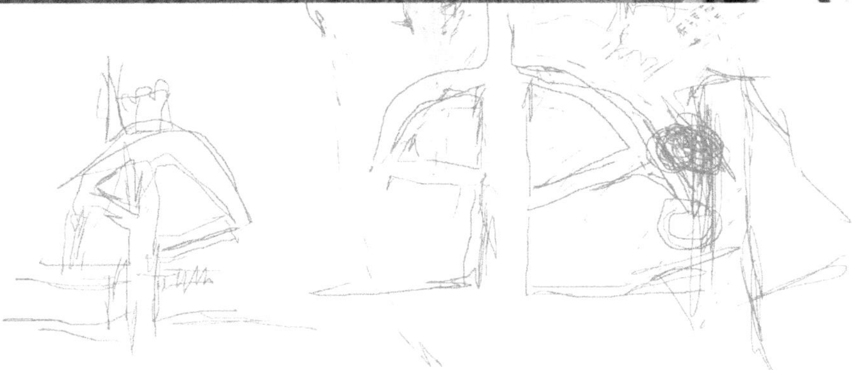

NOTES / NOTIZEN

[EDITING] — [VIDEO] KLAPPE

VIDEO — [SPEECH]

[DRAWING] — [TEXT]

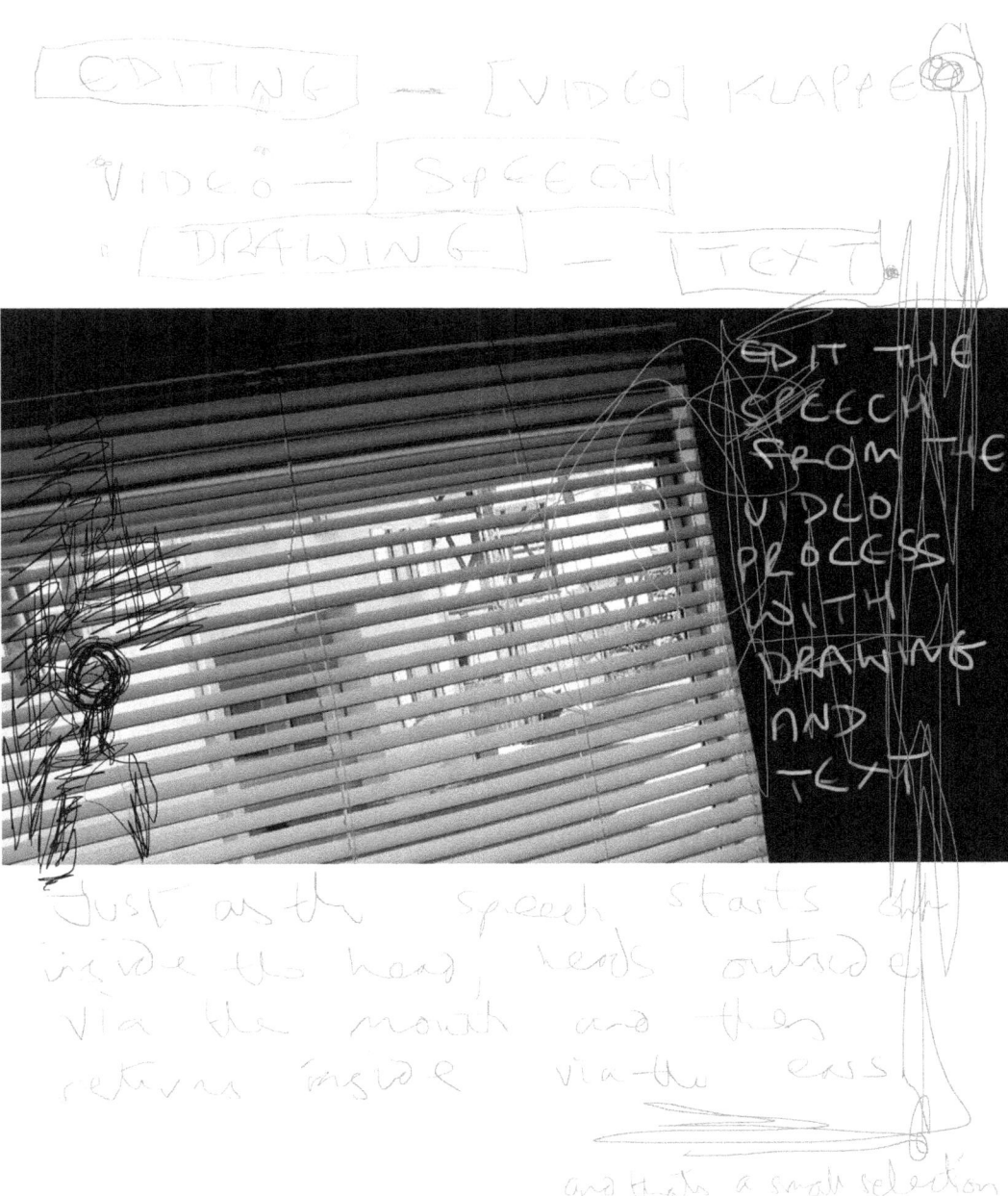

EDIT THE SPEECH FROM THE VIDEO PROCESS WITH DRAWING AND TEXT

Just as the speech starts own
inside the head, heads outside
via the mouth and then
returns inside via the ears

and that a small selection

BIOGRAPHY

Kate Pelling is a British artist based in Germany. Kate Pelling's research-led practice consists of video, drawing and text. Kate Pelling studied at Wirral Metropolitan College, Birkenhead (2003), Wimbledon School of Art, London (2004), and Birkbeck, University of London (2008). She has exhibited extensively in the UK and the USA, and also in Bulgaria, Canada, Germany, Italy, Lithuania, Portugal, and Switzerland. Kate Pelling's first book, *A Relational [Video] Grammar: Extrapolation* was published by Fifth Floor Publications in 2013.

BIOGRAFIE

Kate Pelling ist eine in Deutschland lebende britische Künstlerin.
Kate Pellings forschungsgeleitete Vorgehensweise beinhaltet Video, Zeichnungen und Text. Kate Pelling studierte am Wirral Metropolitan College, Birkenhead (2003), an der Wimbledon School of Art, London (2004) und an der Birkbeck, University of London (2008). Sie hat ihre Werke in umfangreichen Ausstellungen in Großbritannien und den USA sowie Bulgarien, Kanada, Deutschland, Italien, Litauen, Portugal und der Schweiz ausgestellt. Kate Pellings erstes Buch, *A Relational [Video] Grammar: Extrapolation* wurde 2013 von Fifth Floor Publications veröffentlicht.

ACKNOWLEDGEMENTS

I would like to thank Nathan Evans, Dr. Paul Ryan, Otelo M Fabião, Hazel Pelling, Dr. Aaron McPeake, Jim Irvin's voice, Dr. Hayley Newman, Dr. Linda Sandino and Jordan Baseman for their continuing support. Further thanks goes to Jutta Imelda Kanneberger, Christoph Käppeler, Oliver Steinhoff, Becca Permar and Jessa Rianelli. Thank you also to my new muse, he is wonderful but will have to remain anonymous for now.

Thank you to Tina Banerjee Chittom for translating the *Introduction*, *Biography* and *Acknowledgements* of this publication. Thank you to InterTran (www.tranexp.com) for the digital translation of the sections titled *Transcription of Speech/Transkription Von Sprach*.

This publication is dedicated to the memory of my brothers, John and Stuart Pelling

DANKSAGUNGEN

Ich möchte mich bei Nathan Evans, Dr. Paul Ryan, Otelo M Fabião, Hazel Pelling, Dr. Aaron McPeake, der Stimme von Jim Irvin, Dr. Hayley Newman, Dr. Linda Sandino und Jordan Baseman für ihre fortlaufende Unterstützung bedanken. Ich bedanke mich auch bei Jutta Imelda Kanneberger, Christoph Käppeler, Oliver Steinhoff, Becca Permar und Jessa Rianelli. Danke auch an meine neue Muse, er ist wunderbar, doch noch kann sein Name nicht verraten werden.

Danke an Tina Banerjee Chittom für die Übersetzung der *Einleitung*, *Biographie* und *Danksagungen* dieser Veröffentlichung. Danke an InterTran (www.tranexp.com) für die digitale Übersetzung der Abschnitte mit den Titeln *Transcription of Speech/ Transkription Von Sprach*.

Diese Veröffentlichung ist dem Andenken meiner Brüder John und Stuart Pelling gewidmet.

FIFTH FLOOR PUBLICATIONS

Fifth Floor Publications is based in London, UK and Frankfurt am Main, Germany. Founded in 2012, Fifth Floor Publications is a publisher of artists' film and video, either in the form of artists' works as books (digital and hard copy) or videos (online and DVD). Previously published titles include *A Relational [Video] Grammar: Extrapolation* by Kate Pelling (2013).

FIFTH FLOOR PUBLICATIONS

Fifth Floor Publications hat ihren Sitz in London, Großbritannien und Frankfurt am Main, Deutschland. Fifth Floor Publications, der 2012 gegründet wurde, ist ein Verlag für Künstlerfilme und Videos, entweder in Form von Künstlerwerken wie Bücher (digital und in Papierform) oder Videos (online und DVD). Unter anderem wurde der Titel *A Relational [Video] Grammar: Extrapolation* von Kate Pelling (2013) herausgegeben.